Development Ireland

Development Ireland

Contemporary Issues

Edited by

Peter Shirlow

Pluto Press

First published 1995 by
Pluto Press
345 Archway Road
London N6 5AA

British Library Cataloguing in Publication Data
A catalogue record for this book is available from
the British Library

Library of Congress Cataloging in Publication Data
Development Ireland: contemporary issues/edited by Peter Shirlow.
p. cm.
Includes bibliographical references and index.
ISBN 0–7453–0999–2
1. Ireland—Economic conditions. 2. Northern Ireland—Economic conditions. 3. European Union countries—Economic conditions—Regional disparities. I. Shirlow, Peter.
HC260.5.D48 1995
330.9415—dc20 95–5095
CIP

ISBN 0 7453 0999 2 hardback

99 98 97 96 95 5 4 3 2 1

Designed and produced for Pluto Press by
Chase Production Services, Chipping Norton, OX7 5QR
Typeset from author's disk by Stanford DTP Services
Printed in the EC by TJ Press, Padstow, England

'The people of Ireland, gradually replaced by machinery in the north, and by sheep-walks in the south, though even the sheep in that unhappy country are decreasing, it is true, not at so rapid a rate as the men.'

Karl Marx, *Inaugural Address to the First International*, 1864.

Contents

Acknowledgement

This volume was inspired by papers presented to the *Economic Change and Peripherality* Conference held at Queen's University Belfast in 1993. We wish to thank all the people who participated in and attended this conference. In the spirit of the contextual approach that provides the main theme of the chapters in this book, I would also like to acknowledge the important roles played by other social scientists working in this area of analysis. It is important that social scientists concerned with the nature of social and economic marginalisation continue to stand against the injustices so common in our world today.

Thanks also go to proofreaders and typists. Finally I would like to thank the Queen's University Publications Fund which provided necessary financial backing for this venture.

Abbreviations

BUA	Belfast Urban Area
CAP	Common Agricultural Policy
CEC	Commission of the European Communities
CSF	Community Support Framework
DED	Department of Economic Development
DSO	Dublin Stationery Office
EC	European Community
ERM	Exchange Rate Mechanism
ESRI	Economic and Social Research Institute
EU	European Union
FDI	Foreign Direct Investment
GDP	Gross Domestic Product
GNP	Gross National Product
HRM	Human Resource Management
ICTU	Irish Congress of Trade Unions
IDA	Industrial Development Authority
IDB	Industrial Development Board
ITGWU	Irish Transport and General Workers Union
J-I-T	Just-In-Time
LEDU	Local Economic Development Unit
NESC	National Economic and Social Council
NICs	Newly Industrialising Countries
NIEC	Northern Ireland Economic Council
NIERC	Northern Ireland Economic Research Council
NFR	Neo-Fordist Regime
OECD	Organisation for Economic Cooperation and Development
PCW	Programme for Competitiveness and Work
PPRU	Population and Planning Research Unit
SEM	Single European Market
SIPTU	Services Industrial Professional Trade Union
TNCs	Transnational Corporations
UK	United Kingdom

Notes on Contributors

James Anderson teaches Geography at the Open University, Milton Keynes, England. He is the editor of *The Rise of the Modern State* (Wheatsheaf, 1986) and recently co-edited *A Global World?* (Oxford University Press, forthcoming).

Prionnsias Breathnach teaches Geography at St Patrick's College, Maynooth, County Kildare, Ireland. He has written widely on Ireland's position within the new international division of labour in the journals *Antipode* and *Geoforum*, and has contributed to the book *Contemporary Irish Migration* (Geographical Society of Ireland, 1991) and has recently edited *Irish Tourist Development* (Geographical Society of Ireland, 1994).

Andreas Cebulla is a research officer with the Northern Ireland Economic Research Centre, Belfast. He is presently working on an evaluation of urban policy in Northern Ireland.

Honor Fagan teaches Sociology at the University of Durban-Westville, South Africa.

James Goodman is a research officer in the Geography Department, Open University, Milton Keynes, England.

Liam Greenslade is a research officer in the Institute of Irish Studies, Liverpool. He has written extensively on the Irish community in Britain and has contributed to the *Irish Studies Review* and the book *The Irish in the New Communities* (Leicester University Press, 1992).

Douglas Hamilton is a senior research officer with the Northern Ireland Economic Development Office, Belfast. He has contributed to *The Economy of Northern Ireland* (Lawrence and Wishart, 1993) and *The Irish Economy* (Pluto Press, 1993)

Ronnie Munck teaches Sociology at the University of Durban-Westville, South Africa. He is the author of *The Irish Economy* (Pluto Press, 1993).

Jim Smith teaches Sociology at Queen's University Belfast. He has written widely on the socio-political and cultural developments in Ireland and has contributed to *Ireland's Histories* (Routledge, 1991) and *Ireland: Divided Nation, Divided Class* (Ink Links, 1980).

Peter Shirlow teaches Geography in the School of Geosciences, Queen's University Belfast. He has written widely on the political economy of Ireland and has contributed to *Population Migration and the Changing World Order* (Wiley, 1994) and *Migration and Restructuring within Europe* (Belhaven, 1994).

Paul Sweeney is a senior research officer with the Services Industrial Professional Technical Union, Dublin. He is the co-author of *Jobs and Borrowing* (Socialist Economists, 1985).

Jim Walsh teaches Geography at St Patrick's College, Maynooth, County Kildare, Ireland. He is closely involved with the Regional Studies Association and has co-edited *Eu Leader I initiative in Ireland* (Department of Agriculture, 1994) and *Population in Ireland: A Census Atlas* (University College Dublin, 1987).

Tables

Introduction

PETER SHIRLOW

Contemporary Development Issues in Ireland

The purpose of this book is to explore and explain the limitations of contemporary development policies in both Northern Ireland and the Republic of Ireland. Both economies are usually treated separately although their socio-economic convergence, due to the impact of the Single European Market (SEM) and the continued peripheralisation of both economies within Europe, provides strong support for a more inclusive-oriented analysis.[1] Unfortunately, the multiple crises facing the two economies have produced few coherent or critical responses which examine the limitations of development policies both north and south of the border. The lack of public debate concerning contemporary socio-economic issues has also meant that the conventional economic orthodoxy promoted within both economies has been prodigiously unyielding to public challenge and accountability (Kirby, 1988).

In challenging the dominance of conventional economic analysis the contributors to this book adopt the supposition that socio-economic development, in whatever form, engenders difficulties, in that fundamental deficiencies in social organisation are continually reproduced or modified. In Ireland, the extent of these fundamental deficiencies is both prevalent and widespread. A systematic examination of Irish society is developed within this book which demonstrates that the contemporary structure of economic development is characterised by inherent limitations within and between the industrial and social spheres. One of the central limitations of economic development policies has been the failure of both states to challenge the extent of inequality within social conditions. Inequality is not a recent phenomenon but its content and form have been dramatically altered by the heterogeneity of capitalist-led development. The heterogeneous nature of change promotes two interlaced imperatives of analysis within this volume: an examination of contemporary socio-economic conditions and a theoretical account concerning the emergence and sustainment of such conditions.

The main characteristic of development policies has been the faith placed, by policy makers throughout Ireland, in neo-liberal economics and a modernist ideology which upholds the ideals of free trade and free enterprise (O'Hearn, 1993). The result of supporting such economic paradigms has been the promotion of a restricted and overtly ahistorical vision of development which not only relegates social issues but also abstains from examining important cultural and political mechanisms (Peet, 1991). In challenging the positivist and inverted focus of development policies, within the two economies, the contributors have sought to provide a critical analysis which applies a broader societal perspective of uneven development and inequality within Irish society.

The starting point for such a critical political economy approach is the supposition that a complex interplay between domestic and external forces conditions the nature of socio-economic development and transformation within contemporary capitalist societies (Lipietz, 1992; Mjoset, 1992; Munck, 1993). External relations have generally been determined by the nature of global capitalism and Ireland's geographical and historical transformation within this system. It must be stressed, however, that the negative aspects of Ireland's integration into the global economy should not be overemphasised at the expense of examining the state-sponsored context of capital accumulation and a whole range of domestic socio-political impediments and institutional relationships which have also retarded Ireland's socio-economic development (McAuley, 1994).

In general terms, contemporary economic development policies in Ireland have been tied to the maximisation of output growth and the continual modernisation and disclosure of productive forces. There is of course nothing unique about two small peripheral economies fully engaged within the capitalist global economy promoting the free play of market forces and the ideology of economic modernisation. There is also nothing unique in the promotion of such policies and developmental norms sustaining continual uneven development of the two economies within the contemporary global context. Uneven development is a relative term which refers to how the spatial organisation of socio-economic phenomena are highly differentiated due to the spatial unevenness of capitalist development. More specifically the term refers to the development and organisation of economies in relation to spatial divisions of labour, new forms of capital penetration and the effects of accumulation and devalorisation (Mjoset, 1992). However, uneven development reflects far more than simply the lack of geographical evenness in capitalist growth; rather it comprises the comprehensive manner of capitalist development, and refers to the distortion or subversion of development. As such, uneven development refers to a socially or spatially restricted process of development which is underpinned by exploitative and unequal power relationships producing profound social contradictions (Peet, 1991).

As noted above, the nature of uneven development within Ireland can be gauged in both external and internal terms. In global terms the development of the two economies has been nothing but mediocre. The gap in social prosperity between Ireland and western Europe has widened as more prosperous nations have come to control a greater share of industrial and social wealth.[2] The failure to increase purchasing power parities, in relation to other European Union (EU) (formerly the European Community) member states, has also been accompanied by an 8.1 per cent fall in average domestic incomes over the same period (Chomney, 1993). The continual peripheralisation and uneven development of the Irish economy within the European context bear testimony to the organisational activity of contemporary capitalism and its continual division of Europe, between powerful core regions and weak peripheral regions dependent upon EU funds and foreign direct investment. In relation to the other EU member states the Irish economy has gained the dubious honour of being the only economy in which the present level of employment is lower than in the 1920s (OECD, 1993). Ireland's exceptional status within western Europe is the combined result of continued rationalisation of indigenous and foreign-controlled industries and somewhat unique demographic pressures.

Within the European context the supposition has been that regional convergence and the development of peripheral economies is achievable only through the creation of a single market, the removal of trade barriers and the increased exposure of peripheral economies to market forces. In reality, the pursuit of regional convergence through the free flows of factors of production and price stability has created regional divergence resulting from a new economic liberalisation of Europe tied to an intensified mode of industrial competition (Lipietz, 1992). For peripheral regions, such as Ireland, the potential to engage positively within this new competitive mode of industrial organisation is hampered by the fact that the Irish economy is so underdeveloped that it possesses neither the productive resources nor the political power necessary to compete fairly. In internal terms, the uneven development of the Irish economy is characterised by extended social marginalisation due to the combined growth of poverty, unemployment and emigration, and an inequitable distribution of social opportunity. The pursuit of a development model tied to free market policies has continually failed to resolve distributional conflicts. The failure to redistribute wealth more equitably has created a host of unsavoury social conditions. In the Republic, the collapse in the social homogeneity of urban and rural working class localities is in clear contradiction to the conspicuous wealth evident in middle and upper income suburban areas. In Northern Ireland, high levels of social dislocation have been motivating factors for both Republican and Loyalist paramilitaries. The growth in unemployment has in turn created a contemporary social dualism between a wealthy local elite who enjoy the benefits of consumer indulgence and relative job security at the expense of a marginalised low income class whose lives are dependent upon social welfare and emigration, and whose communities are adversely affected by declining social coherence (Kirby, 1988). Moreover, low income groups receive an insignificant share of the wealth presently being created, not solely due to unemployment growth and the subsequent inability to receive wages, but also to extreme income inequality. As such the development of productive and social forces has been tied to a clear demarcation of class interests and opportunities. Both the adoption of the contemporary process of economic development and its failure to challenge the perpetuation of social heterogeneity divides and impedes the development of a more equitable Irish society. A glance at class, gender and regional disparities reveals how fragmented Irish society actually is. The present traditional responses toward social dislocation and the future of the economy assume that a significant growth in output automatically implies socio-economic development. Such simplistic assumptions continually refuse to examine development in terms of fulfilling human needs through challenging social marginalisation, the extension of poverty and the provision of meaningful and satisfying work (Mjoset, 1992).

The realities of the Irish economy are essentially more complex than assumed by such conventional economic analysis; a complexity which is exacerbated by the coexistence of two economies on the island of Ireland. The economies differ in both sectoral and institutional terms, although a similarity exists in that both economies have singularly failed to stimulate improved employment opportunities and material conditions for a significant section of their respective populations. There is no doubting that the two economies continually provide a livelihood for fewer and fewer people even though their respective governments spend billions annually in order to stimulate capital investment and economic development. In both instances, increasing state-sponsorship of the economy has clearly sustained profit-making and output growth but not sustainable employment growth or an extension of socio-economic opportunity (Gudgin, 1992; Kennedy, 1993a). If we view the performance of the two economies in unison throughout the twentieth century we come across a distinct paradoxical development pattern. Living standards have increased four-fold since the 1920s, an increase which has been paralleled by meaningful social progression in the form of substantial improvements in education, health and housing provision. However, at the same time, homelessness, unemployment, emigration and welfare dependence have increased dramatically. As such, the continual reproduction of social inequality highlights the uneven nature of contemporary development processes. In order to fully understand how the interaction of social and economic conditions determine an unsatisfactory development profile, it is essential to establish the nature and extent of structural impediments evident within the two economies.

A Socio-economic Profile of Ireland

The underdevelopment of the Republic's economy prior to independence was a feature of British domination, the evolution of the capitalist world system and the subsequent divisive nature of the international division of labour within Europe. The contemporary form of uneven development has been shaped since the 1950s by the Republic's reintegration within the global economy, the evolution of neo-Fordist relations of production and the Republic's intermediate position within the New International Division of Labour. Reintegration, in this instance, was achieved through the abandonment of economic nationalism in favour of a pseudo-cosmopolitanism and almost total subservience to international capital (Smyth, 1991). The removal of the previous protectionist regime of economic development was based on a development path linked to industrialisation through invitation and outward-oriented growth (Munck, 1993). The main form of industrialisation during this period has been characterised by a disarticulated form of location based on fragmented production units and the decentralisation of manual execution (Perrons, 1981). The attraction of Foreign Direct Investment (FDI) has been a central strategy within the Neo-Fordist Regime (NFR). Although both economies have relied heavily upon foreign investment as a developmental structure, the Republic's continued and unfettered allegiance toward FDI has been more pronounced and ceaselessly illustrated by the growth in foreign capital ownership and the free importation of means of production and exportation of profits (Sklair, 1988). The demise of the indigenous sector and the promotion of export-led development during the NFR have meant that Transnational Corporations (TNCs) have come to play a decisive role within the Republic's economy. By 1989 over half (56 per cent) of the total gross output of manufacturing industries and 70 per cent of net output was controlled by TNCs (Department of Industry and Commerce, 1993).

It would appear that the main role of the Irish state within the NFR, as a facilitator of accumulatory activities of both the foreign and indigenous bourgeoisie, has been relatively successful. In relation to economic growth indicators the NFR has been characterised by improved terms of trade and significant growths in Gross National Product (GNP) and Gross Domestic Product (GDP), and a marked increase in labour productivity per employed person. For example, between 1981 and 1993 the value of GNP and exports grew by 61 per cent and £7152 billion respectively (Banc Ceannais Na hEireann, 1992; OECD, 1993).

The development of productive forces and the evolution of a more efficient externally dominated economy have, however, led to a host of negative relationships which have hindered a more utilitarian mode of socio-economic development. The augmentation of foreign control over the economy has contributed to a diminution of state sovereignty over political and economic forces. The externally owned sector's domination of employment flows and technology shifts has reduced state control over social goals, social welfare and economic policy direction (Munck, 1993). Such high levels of dependency and the uncontrollable nature of FDI means that the Republic does not fully participate in the development of global production practices and the contemporary process of economic innovation. Furthermore, it is clear that in relation to profits, the externally controlled sector pays insignificant taxes and generally repatriates a significant proportion of their profits (Gibbons, 1988). By 1993 profit repatriation in the Republic stood at 14.7 per cent of GDP (OECD, 1993). Profit repatriation is so significant that it could be argued that the Republic's healthy economic growth indicators, relating to GNP and export growth, are wholly unreliable as a guide to the nature of the Republic's economy. The Republic does not have a 'real' trade surplus, whatever official figures indicate. If the official export surplus were to be calculated net of profit repatriation for the externally controlled sector there would actually be a significant trade deficit.

The continual extraction of surplus from the Republic's economy has been accompanied by a growth in state indebtedness. In 1993 the Irish debt burden was equivalent to 92.2 per cent of GDP and its servicing was equal to 24 per cent of total government expenditure (OECD, 1993). At its height in 1986, debt as a percentage of GDP was 116.8 per cent. The burden of the Republic's huge national debt impedes all attempts to create a new development strategy and furthers free marketering and a reduction in social welfare expenditure. The augmentation of the debt burden during the 1980s further highlights the dichotomy between government expenditure and substantial profit growth rates among TNCs. The continual dependence upon TNCs is vitally important for the very survival of the Irish state, and as such heralds the failure of the state to create a non-dependent development regime. The continual dependence upon FDI is tied to the inability of the Republic's bourgeoisie to create a sustainable programme of industrialisation which would support present employment levels. TNCs supply wages and incomes which maintain significant sections of the Republic's population and in so doing removes the potential of extensive class hostilities. In the Republic the structural limitations evident among indigenous-owned industries have produced high levels of financial, technological and trade dependence upon the externally owned sector (Shirlow and Shuttleworth, 1994).

Another negative aspect relating to the contemporary mode of development is the incompatibility between significant growths in gross output and productivity and the continual expansion of unemployment (OECD, 1993). This failure to translate output growth into employment is a symptom of accumulatory activities within contemporary capitalism and can be understood as resulting from changes within the labour process that have promoted the raising of productivity levels, the intensification of work and the deskilling or even enskilling of labour. Competitive pressures have led TNCs continually to re-evaluate employment policies, which in turn have directly affected previous labour market structures and employment totals. Increased global competition, with a premium on price, quality and responsiveness to customer needs, has promoted rapidly changing technologies which emphasise the need for flexible and adaptable organisations and workforces. A distinct supply-side crisis is presently underway and is reflected in the decline of the position of manual workers employed by TNCs (SIPTU, 1993).

In socio-economic terms the Republic's unemployment rate at 21.1 per cent is at a record high and stands at twice the EU average (OECD, 1993). Employment, as a percentage of the total population, has fallen from 35.7 per cent in 1970 to 31.1 per cent in 1993. During the same period there has been an eight per cent fall in active labour force participation and a 27 per cent growth in aggregate unemployment (OECD, 1993). The structural severity of unemployment has also been reflected in the extent and composition of long-term unemployment.[3] In comparison with other EU states, the Republic has produced the highest growth in long-term unemployment from a below average 36.7 per cent in 1983 to the third highest rate of 63.7 per cent in 1994 (Shirlow and Shuttleworth, 1994). The failure to produce an accumulatory regime capable of sustaining employment and domestic income growth has also been tied to the continuation and extension of class disparities and the perpetuation of a highly conservative political structure controlled by bourgeois property interests (Smyth, 1991). The capitalist class is heavily subsidised through low corporation tax, massive state subsidies and relatively low levels of personal taxation (Chomney, 1993).[4] In addition to tax breaks, there is a range of state-sponsored agencies which are almost entirely devoted to sustaining the private sector. Such a high level of state subsidisation of industry has been centred upon the creation of a politically dependent capitalist-based property-owning class whose activities are largely predicated upon the exploitation of its relationship with Fianna Fail. The middle classes have also managed to preserve and further their position by a near monopoly of access to higher education and the professional trades, whereas the Republic's working class has continually borne the brunt of increased dependence on welfare assistance and emigration (O'Hearn, 1993). However, such high levels of social marginalisation have not promoted a political structure capable of removing the pro-bourgeoisie dominance of Irish politics (Kirby, 1988). The failure to promote a more radical political system has been influenced by the distinct nature of the contemporary socio-political system. High levels of out-migration and social dislocation have produced a sense of fatalism among the Republic's working class who have accepted emigration and unemployment as an alternative to challenging what it deems to be an unmoveable and dominant political order. As such the political system has not supported coherent and systematic alternatives capable of tackling the nature of social dislocation. In overall terms, the low level of capital retention, the failure of the Republic to control its own productive resources and the growth of a distinct socially objective mode of accumulation have hindered the elaboration of a more equitable development process.

In Northern Ireland similar socio-structural weaknesses exist, although the process of economic restructuring has run in parallel with high levels of deindustrialisation and socio-religious conflict. It is accurate to argue that the socio-economic crisis that affects the Northern Irish economy is more endemic than that evident in the Republic, due to the mitigation of its viability as a distinct economic entity. Deindustrialisation and the high levels of dependence upon the state sector bear testimony to the extent of economic decline endured in Northern Ireland since the Second World War. At present labour market conditions are extremely inhospitable and are complicated by high levels of religious discrimination. In effect social dislocation is evident not only in class terms but also in terms of religious affiliation (Teague, 1993a). The subsequent politicisation of the labour market and the dispute over discrimination and social opportunity have in turn exacerbated the divide between pro-British and pro-Irish sections of the North's population. The lack of political consensus over socio-economic issues is complicated even further by the nature of Northern Ireland's democratic deficit. The development agencies that do exist are largely unaccountable due to their administration being the sole preserve of the Northern Ireland Office. The combination of bureaucratisation and the sectarian nature of politics in Northern Ireland has meant that the collapse in the economy has not produced a coherent political response capable of challenging the nature of inequality and social dislocation. As such, the continual failure of development policies is closely tied to low levels of accountability due to the nature of socio-political conflict.

Northern Ireland's socio-economic plight has been closely tied to the relative economic decline of the United Kingdom (UK). On virtually every socio-economic indicator Northern Ireland has performed below average in comparison to all other UK regions.

Recent data on GDP and unemployment further illustrates Northern Ireland's continuing socio-economic disadvantage as a region of the EU. At present unemployment is the twelfth highest of all EU regions while GDP per capita between 1988 and 1993 was 24.4 per cent lower than the EU average (Shirlow, 1994). Unemployment rose from 4.3 per cent in 1974 to 14.2 per cent in 1994. This has been paralleled by an employment shortfall of 28.9 per cent between 1971 and 1986, and a 42 per cent decline in manufacturing employment since 1970 (Borooah, 1993). Between 1980 and 1994 employment among indigenous-controlled manufacturing companies declined by 22.1 per cent in Northern Ireland (McCluskey, 1994). The indigenous-controlled manufacturing base in Northern Ireland is continually handicapped by a lack of innovation, high levels of over-specialisation in declining low-value added sectors, reduced levels of investment, grant dependence and a loss of industrial competitiveness. The combination of these structural impediments has continually retarded the development of an indigenous-controlled post-Fordist-based economy centred upon market-led innovation and self-reliant productive systems (Clulow and Teague, 1993). The removal of such systemic distortions among indigenous-controlled industry is further handicapped by a low-skills base which provides neither the constructional dynamics nor the skill levels necessary to engender a more competitive and technologically sophisticated development structure; a structure which is also constrained by low levels of cross-border trade and the religious polarisation of the workforce and business community in Northern Ireland. Furthermore, the failure of indigenous-controlled industry to emulate the more successful post-Fordist model of development centred upon flexible automation and the full integration of research and development condemns Northern Ireland to a peripheral role which is incapable of challenging the uneven distribution of technical and social progress within the EU (Perrons, 1992).

What is clearly evident is that the systemic distortions created by alterations in labour market and productive structures have not been addressed by contemporary policy making structures. Disequilibrium within social conditions is matched by policy making which is incapable of redressing the formation of extended social inequality. In both the Republic and Northern Ireland it is patently obvious that the contemporary nature of institutional governance is incapable of overriding the vagaries of contemporary capital accumulation strategies. What we are left with is a general failure by policy makers to acknowledge the extent to which new productive techniques and labour market structures have altered previous social and employment relationships.[5] It is clear that present development policies throughout Ireland are nothing more than aspirational: they continually assume that the protracted support of economic growth structures will somehow automatically produce widespread socio-economic benefits. In challenging the myopia of development initiatives in Ireland, it is important to promote a robust examination of Irish society which stresses the pragmatic and epistemological indivisibility of method, theory and empirical research. In promoting such an inclusive analytical framework the contributors to this volume have chosen to emphasise particular aspects of contemporary Irish society which utilise and interpret the nature of socio-economic change and development policies. In addressing the issues outlined above the book is divided into two interlinked sections. Chapters one to five examine the effect of both present and future development policies upon the structure of the Irish economy within a general European perspective. Such conditions are related to an examination concerning technological change, alterations within the mode of production, the role of the state and the new international division of labour. Chapters six to eight are primarily concerned with providing a theoretical analysis of the socio-cultural impediments created by historically conditioned and contemporary forces of social reproduction within Irish society.

Chapters 1–5: Peripherality, Policy and Europe

In analysing development policies, both Breathnach and Hamilton challenge the conceptual grasp of policy making in Ireland due to the continual support given to conventional economic analysis. Criticism is directed at policy making structures which continually fail to provide institutional frameworks and developmental norms capable of supporting progressive socio-economic innovation. Both authors agree that development policies have failed to engender a vibrant indigenous-controlled sector which encourages more innovative and competitive post-Fordist-based industries, capable of reacting to market volatility through extending product ranges and the stimulation of clusters of interlinked industrial activity. In the Republic, according to Breathnach, the limited range of institutional thinking and the nature of the government's reaction to the *Culliton Report* (1992) have meant that the type of autocentric development which is tied to supporting interlinked and post-Fordist clusters of industrial activity has been undermined by a fixation with ahistorical short-term planning initiatives. For Hamilton, increased North–South trade and industrial activity are proposed as a framework capable of stimulating economies of scale and industrial clustering among indigenous industries. An increase in intra-island trade would, it is argued, stimulate international competitiveness, reduce ineffective competition between development agencies and stimulate a larger pool of innovation and technological know-how. The validity of a new developmental model will of course be tied to the institutional nature of governance throughout Ireland. Anderson and Goodman also support the notion that a new inter-regional model of development should be applied in order to stimulate an autonomous agglomeration economy, especially due to the nature of EU regionalism which is presently strengthening the economies of core post-Fordist-type regions. However, they are wary of the feasibility of producing such structures in the light of the misguided and centralised nature of policy making and the extent of political violence in Northern Ireland. For example, the centrality of the two states in Ireland and the lack of formal support for such an initiative have hampered cross-border cooperation. Furthermore, the failure to produce a distinct political framework capable of supporting cross-border trade is in itself the main obstacle to achieving socio-economic unification and therefore a more innovative form of socio-economic development.

Emerging regionalism and the extent of fiscal support supplied through EU funds are central issues within Walsh's analysis of economic development within the Republic of Ireland. As Walsh makes clear, a coherent form of socio-economic development is only possible when territorial and functional needs are integrated. However, such integration is impeded due to a combined lack of flexibility in planning, a failure to support democratic forms of partnership and a lack of commitment to the overall process of planning for sub-regional development. Sweeney's analysis is primarily concerned with the failure of productive reorganisation and free market ideology to stimulate the quality of human resources and innovation within Irish industry. As such he argues that post-Fordist production techniques should not be tied solely to providing productivity gains and wage reductions but should also support the active participation of labour through the adoption of new ways of working. Workplace reorganisation, it is argued, could be achieved through a collective model of development centred upon increased workforce participation and labour emancipation; an approach which readopts the basic tenet of social democracy and consensus and which attacks the illusionary nature of neo-liberal planning initiatives. Free market ideology and its inherent social contradictions are an unrealistic model of development due to the continual failure of industry to encourage the talents and skills base of a highly educated Irish workforce.

Chapters 6–8: Culture, Class and Theory

Two contributions within this volume are clearly linked to spatial and politically sensitive analyses of crisis and social injustice within Ireland. For Smith and Cebulla the manipulation of the urban class structure and the attempt to regulate the armed conflict in Belfast have truncated socio-economic development and in so doing have heightened the nature of social inequality and socio-religious animosity between the Catholic and Protestant working-class communities. Post-industrial planning initiatives have produced a regeneration strategy which has favoured and facilitated the development of a distinct middle-income group at the expense of a marginalised urban working class. Greenslade adopts the theme, spelt out by Smith and Cebulla, that the post-colonial nature of Irish society has also impeded socio-economic development. The legacy of a sectarian statelet in Northern Ireland and the failure of the native bourgeoisie to promote a sustainable and equitable socio-cultural project throughout Ireland have been detrimental. Furthermore, the continual importance attached to nation building and national identity is in itself a developmental block, as it plays an overdetermining and divisive role within Irish society.

Munck and Fagan provide the final chapter which re-emphasises the collective responsibility of theorists to consider the plurality between theory and society, and to recognise that the importance of theory rests not upon its binary opposition to conventional analysis but also upon its own normative ideological underpinnings. Munck and Fagan also stress that commitment and relevance are only valid when they are tied to a spirit of criticism which is prepared constantly to adjust and adapt to conceptual categories and emerging historical conditions. Their view of theoretical adoption also challenges the 'left' in Ireland to engage in the development debate not as an antithesis of conventional economics but as transformatory agent centred upon a reconstruction of development discourses and the promotion of democratic involvement.

Notes

1. Throughout this chapter the term Ireland refers to the island of Ireland.
2. The divergence in social prosperity between the Republic of Ireland and other EU member states is more extreme than is the case with the other three other peripheral regions (Spain, Portugal and Greece), all of whom have improved 'Purchasing Power Parities' ratings by an average of 14.1 per cent during the same period. The better performance of these other areas is due to their rising from a much lower purchasing power base.
3. Long-term unemployed refers to those unemployed for 12 months or longer.
4. The level of state intervention in Ireland is very high in comparison to other EU and main competitor states. In 1993 the Irish state spent an equivalent of 9.1 per cent of GNP on industry compared to an EU average of 3.1 per cent (Shirlow, 1994).
5. The debate concerning post-industrial flexibility has focused on work and employment relations. Two forms of flexibility are identified. Functional flexibility deals specifically with the organisation of work and the capacity of a firm to adjust the tasks undertaken by productive and technical workers in response to demand and technology alterations. Numerical flexibility refers to the capability of a firm to alter employment and wage levels. The emergence of such distinct forms of flexibility has also been tied to new production techniques and workplace structures centred upon core and peripheral workforces.

1
Uneven Development and Irish Peripheralisation

PRIONNSIAS BREATHNACH

Ireland – both North and South – is commonly perceived and portrayed as constituting a peripheral region, or more accurately two peripheral regions, within a European context. A Synthetic Index of regional indicators (based on productivity and unemployment) compiled by the EC in 1984 placed Northern Ireland second-last and the Republic of Ireland fourth-last of 131 Level II EC regions. The respective index values as a proportion of the EC average were, 35 per cent for Northern Ireland and 42 per cent for the Republic of Ireland. For Hamburg, the region with the highest index, the respective proportions were 23 per cent and 27 per cent (Trimble, 1990). A more sophisticated index published in 1987 showed the Republic's, and more particularly Northern Ireland's, relative position to have improved significantly, but this was mainly due to the effect of EC enlargement. Both parts of Ireland were still more than one standard deviation worse than the EC average, and were the only EC regions outside the Mediterranean area in this category. Ireland's economic peripherality is commonly seen as essentially geographical, i.e. Ireland is located on the margins of a European economy in which economic prosperity and dynamism are strongly concentrated in a core region frequently referred to as the 'Golden Triangle'. Economic opportunity is seen as being a function of accessibility to the external economies offered by this core region (Keeble et al., 1982). From this point of view, therefore, geographically peripheral regions such as Ireland face severe disadvantages which account, in large part, for their poor comparative economic performance.

This chapter reviews some conflicting views on how the problem of peripherality should be tackled from an economic policy point of view, with respect specifically to the Republic of Ireland. The conventional economic emphasis on cost minimisation as the key to international competitiveness is dismissed as an inadequate response to the developmental needs of the Irish economy. The need to create integrated export-oriented industrial sectors is advanced, but the steps required to achieve this are considered to be beyond the conceptual grasp of the Irish economics 'establishment'. The findings of an inquiry into why Ireland has failed to create such a structure, where other small European countries have succeeded, are examined. Some ideas on how this deficiency in the Irish economy can be tackled are then presented. Initially, however, the chapter provides a historical backdrop to the current economic situation in Ireland, both North and South.

Peripheral Ireland

The modern similarity between the economic structures of Northern Ireland and the Republic of Ireland hides the fact that, until relatively recently, there were profound differences between them (Walsh, 1979). In the nineteenth century, the Belfast region in particular experienced a form of industrialisation quite similar to that of many other British regions at the time of the Industrial Revolution. This involved the creation of a specialised and integrated export-oriented economic complex built around the linen, engineering and shipbuilding industries (O'Malley, 1989). By contrast, the remainder of the island actually experienced a process of deindustrialisation in the early nineteenth century, due mainly to the introduction of free trade with Britain following the 1800 Act of Union, and the centralisation of the linen industry in Belfast. As a consequence, the economy of the South was almost entirely dependent on the production and export of agricultural produce to the British market. The resultant lack of diversification and widespread poverty generated a continuous stream of emigrants, mainly to Britain and the USA. By 1921, the population of the island had been reduced to almost one half of the 1841 level (Kennedy et al., 1988). At the time of partition and the establishment of the Irish Free State (subsequently to become the Republic of Ireland), only ten per cent of the South's workforce were engaged in manufacturing industry (compared with over one third in the North), while over one half were engaged in agriculture (Walsh, 1979).

The twentieth century witnessed the North's industrial base experiencing growing difficulties, due mainly to specialisation in industries which have been in secular decline throughout the UK. Thus, the shipbuilding industry is now but a shadow of its former self, while the linen industry has been all but obliterated. Government attempts in the 1960s to replace these declining industries with imported synthetic fibre plants met with considerable initial success, but ultimately foundered when this sector also experienced structural decline in the 1970s. Meanwhile the political troubles have severely constrained the ability to attract other forms of outside investment. In the South, a policy of developing a manufacturing base through providing protection for infant industries serving the domestic market met with considerable initial success. However, the small size of the Irish market placed limits on long-term growth potential, and the inability to expand into export markets inevitably led to eventual stagnation in the 1950s. With the agricultural sector experiencing rapid contraction, this meant unprecedented emigration rates and major overall population decline.

The resultant crisis forced a reversal of economic policy and a switch to export-oriented industrial growth based on the attraction of foreign investment. This policy worked quite well in the 1960s and 1970s, although the employment gains in the foreign sector were counteracted to a considerable extent by contraction of indigenous industry, especially following EC entry in 1973 and the consequent exposure of Irish industry to external competition. In the 1980s there was an overall fallback in manufacturing employment, although output continued to expand strongly. This pointed to basic weaknesses in the prevailing industrial policy, particularly its emphasis on low-skill assembly work which has proved to be vulnerable to automation, and the failure of foreign branch plants to generate a significant degree of local linkage (Breathnach, 1988). Consequently, the 1980s saw both a build-up of unemployment and a resumption of mass emigration from the Republic of Ireland.

The net effect of these trends has been to create economic structures in both Northern Ireland and the Republic of Ireland which are remarkably similar. In both economies the manufacturing sector is now dominated by overseas firms, which account for about 40 per cent of employment and a higher proportion of output in both cases (Hamilton, 1993). Further, the foreign sector consists of limited-skill branch plants with few local linkages (Borooah, 1993; Telesis Consultancy Group, 1982). This, in turn, is related to high levels of unemployment, typically in the 15–20 per cent range in both parts of the island in the late 1980s (despite on-going net emigration from the two areas). While the tertiary sector now dominates the employment structure of both economies, its growth has fallen short of that required to reduce unemployment rates to EU levels.

Overcoming Peripherality: The Conventional View

The conventional economist's typical prescription for dealing with the problem of Irish peripheralisation is to minimise transport and production costs for Irish-based producers.[1] The Irish government has responded to this prescription in part by allocating a high proportion (over one quarter for the period 1989–93) of EC structural funding to the improvement of transport infrastructure. Regarding production costs, these are generally equated by conventional economists with labour costs. This is not entirely unreasonable since, although the share of wages in total manufacturing input costs has been declining, wages remain the largest single element of these costs on average for all industries (Storper and Walker, 1989). However, to argue, as most conventional economists do, that the minimisation of labour costs is the key to international competitiveness is another matter. Thus, in his regular Saturday column in the *Irish Times* (June 5, 1993), Garret Fitzgerald, formerly an academic economist (and, of course, also a former Irish Prime Minister) argued that the fundamental cause of Ireland's current high level of unemployment was excessive wage levels. Virtually simultaneously, Kieran Kennedy, the influential director of the state-sponsored Economic and Social Research Institute, was arguing much the same thing in the June 1993 issue of the *Irish Banking Review* (Kennedy, 1993a).

The fact is that labour costs in Irish manufacturing industry are already much lower than those of Ireland's main trading partners and have been falling quite significantly in relative terms; by over one third in the 1980s (*Economic Review and Outlook*: various years). Yet this has had no apparent bearing on Irish manufacturing employment which declined overall by eight per cent in the 1980s. One may contrast Fitzgerald's one-dimensional view of the Irish employment problem with an international survey reported in the *Irish Times* (July 9, 1993) which compared 38 countries with respect to 37 different criteria for competitiveness. While Ireland performed best regarding unit labour costs in manufacturing industry, it was placed only thirteenth in terms of overall competitiveness. It is clear that there is a lot more to national economic performance than simple labour costs.

Non-conventional Alternatives

It is evident that the conventional neoclassical emphasis on the minimisation of production and transport costs as the key to success in international markets is of little relevance to the search for possible future routes for Irish economic development policy. Over ten years ago the *Telesis Report* on Irish industrial policy pointed to three broad industrial sectors which could potentially be used as a base for Irish industrial development (Telesis Consultancy Group, 1982). These included, first, activities in which low labour costs could offer competitive advantage; second, activities based on natural resources in which Ireland possesses, or could achieve, comparative advantage; and third, what Telesis called 'complex-factor-cost' industries, or what would nowadays be called 'high-tech' industries, in which the key to competitive advantage is technological organisation or marketing know-how.

Telesis went on to dismiss the first of these: Irish wage levels are already such that Ireland could never conceivably compete with those Third World countries which do actively compete in these industries and where wage costs are extremely low compared with Ireland. As regards high-tech industries, studies show that for these, neither labour nor transport costs are necessarily significant factors in market success. Thus, in a survey of American high-tech firms operating in the west European market, Schoenberger (1990) found product quality and support service to be frequently more important than price as factors influencing potential customers. More specifically, Schoenberger noted that, for most of the firms surveyed, the decision on whether or not to locate a production plant in Europe was not influenced by the cost of exporting to Europe from a US base, since 'transportation costs to Western Europe are not considered a significant barrier to competitiveness' (1990, p. 384). Of course, Ireland already exports very large volumes of high-tech products to continental Europe, and these exports have been growing consistently and rapidly over the last twenty years (Foley, 1991). The problem, as noted earlier, has been that Ireland's strong performance as an industrial producer and exporter has not been translating into spin-off jobs elsewhere in the economy. The reasons for this are by now well known. The burgeoning Irish industrial export sector is dominated by foreign firms which have very limited local linkages, mainly because they import the great bulk of their technology, goods and services, export almost all of their input, and repatriate most of their profits (Breathnach, 1988). As a result, the foreign firm sector does not act as an effective national 'economic base', in that strong export revenues have created very weak spin-offs in the form of residentiary (i.e. non-exporting) industries in the ancillary and consumer sectors (Malecki, 1991).

The problem for Ireland, therefore, is to create a vibrant industrial sector based on indigenous industries sourcing material and service inputs within the Irish economy and capable of penetrating export markets (a similar prescription for Northern Ireland has been put forward in Borooah, 1993). As the possibility of developing an indigenous export base, relying on sectors in which labour costs are a key competitive factor, has already been ruled out, the only other options are to be found in the natural resource or modern technological sectors. The question is: how does one go about creating such industries?

The Non-contribution of Irish Economists

There is little evidence that conventional neoclassical economists can be of much assistance in answering this question. This is because of their very limited range of vision. As Lee has observed, among the Irish economics profession (which is almost entirely neoclassical in orientation), 'The premium is on tunnel thinking, blind to either long-term perspective or lateral linkage' (1989, p. 583). This tunnel thinking is partly reflected in the aforementioned preoccupation with cost minimisation. It is further reflected in a concentration on the behaviour of the individual (whether the individual consumer or the individual firm) as the key to understanding the functioning of the economy. As Griffin and Gurley observe:

> No historian, sociologist, political scientist or anthropologist would systematically ignore all the social formations larger than the nuclear household ... conventional economists ... are alone in trying to understand human phenomena in terms of the behaviour of isolated households. (1985: p. 120)

Conventional economists therefore tend to have little grasp of the broad social structures which constrain and shape the behaviour of individual economic factors. Twenty years ago, Myrdal (1973) criticised economists for playing down such 'non-economic' factors as power relations, social and economic stratification, and institutions (such as religion, culture, law and politics) which act as strong impediments to economic development in underdeveloped countries. This criticism can equally be applied to Irish economists today. We may add that conventional economists have even less grasp of the historical processes which produce these social structures, a direct consequence of what Lee (1989) sees as their fixation with immediate problems and short-term movements and their resultant limited understanding of long-term development processes.

A final factor contributing to the tunnel vision characteristic of Irish economists is their tendency to confine themselves to economic models derived exclusively from the British and American experiences. This is to a certain extent understandable, given the reliance of Irish economists on English-language literature and the fact that many of them have done at least part of their training in Britain or the US. However, this has at least two negative consequences. First, it means that most Irish economists have little knowledge of the economic experiences of other countries, both developed and underdeveloped, and of alternative models deriving from these experiences. Second, both the British and American economies developed in circumstances which are quite different from those which pertained in Ireland. Accordingly, development models deriving from the British and American experience are quite inappropriate to the Irish situation. Despite this, Irish economists tend not to look beyond the British and American economic paradigms, which lead them to recommending prescriptive measures which are at odds with the real development needs of the Irish economy. Moreover, economists of conventional neoclassical orientation account for close on 100 per cent of the personnel in Irish university economics departments and in the research institutions and consultancy firms. In effect neoclassical economists inevitably exert a powerful influence in government circles and, as a consequence, policy makers do not become aware of alternative development options.

The Comparative European Perspective

Despite these layers of blinkers which festoon the Irish economics establishment, a definite beam of light was allowed to penetrate recently in the form of a study commissioned by the National Economic and Social Council with the aim of identifying why a number of other European small open economies have achieved so much more economic success than Ireland. Mjoset's (1992) study was refreshing in his socio-historical analysis which transcended the simple macroeconomic analysis of contemporary macroeconomic indicators. Mjoset's basic finding was that the countries selected for comparative purposes (Sweden, Finland, Denmark, Austria and Switzerland) had all managed to achieve what Amin (1974) defines as 'autocentric' development. This refers to a form of development whose driving force emanates from within the national economies in question, and includes a combination of import-substituting and export-oriented industrialisation. These forms of industrialisation have the effect of generating extensive domestic linkages, leading to the formation of what Mjoset terms 'development blocks' (also referred to by Porter (1990) as 'clusters'), that is, interlinked networks of producers of materials and services in particular sectors. The extensive multipliers generated by this form of development lead to the creation of mass employment, low levels of unemployment and high living standards for the majority of the population. Thus what is produced is a virtuous circle of self-expanding economic growth and development, described by Myrdal (1957) as a process of 'cumulative causation'.

Ireland, by contrast, is characterised by what Amin terms 'extraverted' or 'peripheral' development. This describes a situation where the essential structures of a national economy are determined by external forces, and usually include a high level of dependence on exports of unprocessed primary products and imports of manufactured goods, and/or a high level of external ownership of domestic productive assets. Such an economic structure creates very limited local linkages and multiplier effects and low levels of employment creation. These in turn imply marginalisation of a large proportion of the population among whom very low living standards are the norm.

Deindustrialisation, Marginalisation and Emigration

Mjoset attributes Ireland's extraverted form of development to the deindustrialisation which affected most of Ireland (apart from the northeast) in the early nineteenth century. For Mjoset, the single most important consequence of this process of deindustrialisation and associated marginalisation was the generation of a long-lasting tradition of emigration which is still with us today. In this, Ireland was virtually unique among countries with extraverted economies, due essentially to the propinquity to two of the most rapidly expanding economies of the nineteenth century, Great Britain and the US. Although this has allowed the residual population to enjoy a standard of living which is unusual among extraverted economies, it has stripped Ireland of the dynamic impulses which characterise autocentric forms of development. Mjoset concurs with the view that emigration selectively removes potential innovators and entrepreneurs from the national economy, leading to what Oldham described as the 'survival of the unfittest' (1914, p. 213). Had these people chosen to stay at home rather than emigrate, this, Mjoset believes, would have created social tensions and frictions which would have acted as a positive force for social and economic dynamism. However, they opted instead to leave, thereby facilitating the emergence of dominant social forces and institutions opposed to change, and dependent on the maintenance of emigration for their continued prosperity and domination. As a result, Ireland lacks a 'national system of innovation' such as is found in all countries characterised by autocentric development. In effect, Ireland has failed to engender a national institutional framework which encourages and facilitates the adoption of new ways of doing things.

Vicious Circles of Underdevelopment

Mjoset therefore sees in deindustrialisation, marginalisation and emigration the creation of a vicious circle of continued under-development – Myrdal's cumulative causation process working in reverse. Thus, emigration restricted the growth of the home market (and hence the impetus for import substitution), allowed the emergence of a pastoral bias in agriculture, with a limited capacity for backward linkages, and fostered social structures in the countryside inimical to social progress. These forces have produced a weak national system of innovation, leading to a lack of economic growth, limited employment opportunities, social marginalisation and further emigration, thereby completing the circle. As Mjoset sees it, this vicious circle created an institutional framework which was, if anything, strengthened by the transition to political independence by what was to become the Republic of Ireland. This is reflected in the emergence in the post-colonial period of subsidiary economic and socio-political vicious circles from the initial vicious circle which became established in the colonial period. In the economic sphere, the social structure emanating from the latter period produced a political system which gave primacy to the agrarian interest, leading to the maintenance of the emphasis on cattle exports and a continued dependence on the British market. This lack of diversification has led to the continuation of a weak national system of innovation, which in turn has failed to halt emigration and has preserved an entrenched agrarian-dominated social structure.

In the socio-political sphere, the loss of potentially radical elements via emigration led to the emergence of two 'catch-all' political parties unable to challenge the dominant elements in the conservative social structure and unable to articulate the voice of the marginalised. This again confirms the weakness of the national system of innovation and the continuation of emigration, thus maintaining the circle. Several of the key elements of the institutional structures embedded in Mjoset's vicious circles have declined greatly in influence in the last thirty years. These include the dependence on cattle and beef exports, the dominance of the Catholic Church and the agrarian orientation of the political system. However, for both politicians and the state bureaucracy, innovation remains anathema. The education system continues to inculcate deeply conservative views, particularly among the intelligentsia, and the indigenous business community remains imbued with a 'quick-buck' mentality which is a direct throw-back to the circumstances pertaining in the nineteenth-century agrarian economy.

New institutions have emerged, however, to counter potential tendencies in the direction of radical innovation. These include the penetration of foreign media which continually convey conservative ideologies, growing dependence of the indigenous business community on the foreign-owned industrial sector, and EU subsidies which have played an important role in helping the Irish government to cope with rapidly growing unemployment since the early 1980s.

What are the Real Alternatives?

Having indicated where Ireland went wrong, Mjoset provides no guidelines on how Ireland might break out of these vicious circles. While he cites, apparently approvingly, Gerschenkron's (1962) view that intervention on the part of the state (or the banking system) is a *sine qua non* for effective economic development in late-developing economies, the problem for Ireland is where the impetus for such intervention might come, given the innately conservative nature both of government itself (referring both to the dominant political parties and the state bureaucracy) and of those groups which exert effective political influence on government.

Furthermore there have been very few peripheral countries which have managed to make the transition to autocentric development. The obvious exceptions have been the newly industrialising countries (NICs) of East Asia (Korea, Taiwan and Hong Kong). The recent economic histories of these three countries have been fundamentally different from other so-called NICs (such as Singapore, Brazil and Mexico) in that they have succeeded in creating dominant indigenous industrial sectors with strong local linkages. Henderson (1990) attributes this to the fact that all three possessed governments faced with legitimation crises in the 1950s due either to the threat of rapidly developing neighbours with territorial designs (North Korea and China) or the complete absence of democratic representative government (Hong Kong). These threats, according to Henderson, were sufficiently strong to spur the governments in question to undertake the kinds of radical action required to create autocentric economic structures capable of raising living standards considerably throughout the population. In this, South Korea and Taiwan in particular had the neighbouring model of Japan to draw on. They also, it might be added, lacked the democratic structures which might have stymied the severe measures employed, particularly in the early stages of industrialisation. This is especially the case in relation to wage suppression and poor working conditions, both of which were needed in order to attract foreign technology and gain footholds in export markets.

In the case of Ireland, it could be argued that there was one instance of a legitimation crisis in the 1950s, when mass emigration seriously threatened the continued viability of the state. This did produce a radical response witnessed by the abandonment of de Valera's policy of economic autarky and protectionism. However, whereas the alternative policy of attracting foreign investment may appear at first glance to have been similar to contemporaneous policies being pursued in the East Asian 'tigers', in the case of the latter this was part of a long-term policy designed to create a self-reliant technological capacity, whereas in the case of Ireland foreign investment constituted an end in itself. For more than twenty years foreign investment did manage to keep the economic and political wolf from the Irish government's door. However, foreign investment is no longer delivering the goods, and there is little indication that anybody with political influence in Ireland has a clear notion of where to go from here. This is evident from the public reaction to the *Culliton Report* on industrial policy (Industrial Policy Review Group, 1992). From the viewpoint of this chapter, by far the most important recommendation emanating from this report was the proposal that industrial promotion policy should be oriented towards the fostering of clusters of interlinked industries. This, as we have seen, is an essential ingredient of autocentric development. However, this rather complex dimension was virtually ignored in subsequent political, media and academic comment on the report, which focused instead on the politically juicy elements such as tax reform and the restructuring of state agencies.

Conclusion

One is, therefore, less than sanguine about the prospects of Ireland escaping from its condition of economic peripherality in the foreseeable future. The institutional forces opposed to the requisite change are simply too strong and entrenched. The only conceivable source of political pressure for radical change is the high, and growing, levels of unemployment and low-paid employment. There are signs that these are finally forcing job creation to the top of the government's agenda. However, there is no indication as of yet of the formation of a coherent political movement around this issue. One suspects that a lot depends on the ability of the EU heartland to provide subsidies sufficient to keep such potential mobilisation under wraps. The latest round of enlarged EU Structural Funds, therefore, may have the effect of putting the day of reckoning back at least until the beginning of the coming century.

Note

1. In the remainder of the chapter, the terms 'Irish' and 'Ireland' refer to the Republic of Ireland only.

2

Peripherality and the Political Economy of Northern Ireland

DOUGLAS HAMILTON

Peripherality is commonly presented as a major impediment to economic development, and an issue especially important at a regional level, as in the case of Northern Ireland. However, peripherality is a particularly amorphous and ill-defined concept and can mean quite different things to different people.[1] The most common definition refers to peripherality as an aspect of geographic or spatial location. In this context peripherality is seen as a problem if a region is distant from markets and, more specifically, if transport costs are a significant component of the overall costs of production and distribution. In addition to this rather narrowly defined spatial concept of peripherality there is a substantial literature in regional economics, geography, new theories of international trade, development studies and politics which views peripherality in a changing and arguably more fundamental context. Such views tie peripherality into more general developments taking place in the forms which industrial capitalism adopts internationally, in particular the key economic and political relationships between core and peripheral zones. At a general level these core-periphery relationships are concerned with the hierarchical structure of the global economy and the manner in which countries and regions fit into the political economic regime in terms of relative power and subordination (O'Hearn, 1993). More specifically, and of particular interest here, much of this recent literature refers to the fundamental changes in production processes which have taken place over the last twenty years – the shift from 'Fordist' or mass-production systems to 'post-Fordist' or flexible specialisation techniques (Piore and Sabel, 1984)[2] – and how this impacts on regional development.

This chapter discusses geographic peripherality (here defined largely in terms of transport costs) in relation to Northern Ireland, a view of peripherality which tends to prevail among those who formulate and implement policy. This discussion is then extended to include some wider aspects of economic peripherality. An admittedly simplistic distinction between geographic and economic peripherality is presented, but this is done for the purpose of highlighting the limitations of the policy response to peripherality within Northern Ireland – a key aim of the chapter. Furthermore, the concept of peripherality, and the problems it raises, is used as a way of examining how economic development in Northern Ireland could be improved. This discussion is placed, not just within developments in economic thinking, but also against the background of observed cases of successful regional economies. In conclusion an attempt is made to raise some new perspectives on how the deep economic problems of Northern Ireland might be more effectively approached.

Geographic Peripherality

Peripherality is probably most commonly thought of as a concept related to geographic location. In this context, countries or regions most distant from major markets and centres of population would be considered peripheral. In the case of Northern Ireland, if only looked at in European terms, the region is clearly peripheral. Northern Ireland is situated in the northwest of Europe and is separated from continental Europe by Britain. Since the completion of the Channel Tunnel, Ireland is now the only sizeable part of the EU without a road link to continental Europe. Moreover, it can be argued that on the island of Ireland, the border with the Republic, despite the creation of the Single European Market and the disappearance of custom controls, acts as an important barrier to increased trade and economic activity through the physical, political, militaristic and psychological obstacles that it creates.[3] It is clear, then, that Northern Ireland is an especially peripheral region in Europe, if only in geographic terms. Not surprisingly it is this aspect of peripherality which has been overemphasised in terms of policy adoption. Almost every discussion of the acute economic problems of Northern Ireland mentions peripherality as a key impediment to economic development.[4] The government's so-called 'Pathfinder' document listed Northern Ireland's 'distance penalties' as one of the six root causes of poor performance (Department of Economic Development (DED), 1987). The government's more recent strategy document *Competing in the 1990s* stated Northern Ireland's peripheral location at the edge of the European single market as one of three major constraints on local industry (Department of Economic Development, 1990). The

Northern Ireland Economic Council (NIEC) in a wide-ranging report on economic strategy commented that Northern Ireland by any geographic parameters is wholly peripheral in both a national and European context and that this acts as a major constraint within which government policy has to operate (NIEC, 1991).

While it is generally accepted (it would be difficult to deny) that Northern Ireland is geographically peripheral, there is considerable debate as to the importance of this in impeding economic development and, in particular, industrial activity. Both neo-classical regional economic theory and intuition suggest, other things being equal, that transport costs in a geographically peripheral region will constrain the development of local industry by requiring it to be proportionately more competitive than its rivals (Richardson, 1969). However, there is some debate as to the importance of transport costs in Northern Ireland. Hitchens, Wagner and Birnie (1990) suggest that they are not substantial, while a government study states that transport costs amounted to 10.8 per cent of gross value added (PPRU, 1987). Such an estimate suggests that transport costs may not amount to a significant proportion of overall costs. The conventional or neo-classical approach to peripherality through the minimisation of transport costs is far from sufficient, or even irrelevant, if economic development is to be improved. For example, O'Hearn (1993) in a far more pessimistic perspective on the role of transport infrastructure argues, with some force, that EU transfers, in the case of the Republic of Ireland, while bringing obvious benefits to the local population in terms of improved roads, rail and ports, mainly facilitate the operations of foreign producers on the island.[5] In essence he argues that core areas have always attempted to improve the infrastructure of peripheries by bringing them closer to the productive centres, but that this has been done to enable the core to operate more profitably within the periphery. Fundamentally, O'Hearn's argument is that global capitalism has a strict hierarchical structure and provides limited possibilities for upward mobility for peripheral regions. Core firms and states are said to attain and maintain economic power through the very continuation of regional inequalities. It would seem that there is a mixed, unclear and, to some extent, contradictory picture concerning the importance of transport costs in the Northern Ireland economy. While some studies suggest that transport costs are not a significant component of overall costs to industry, they are, not surprisingly, more important than in other areas of the UK. It seems wise to conclude, therefore, that geographic peripherality in terms of transport costs will continue to be a factor in determining local economic performance. However, the emphasis on geographic (transport related) aspects of peripherality has allowed less attention to be given to other more important economic aspects of peripherality.

Economic Aspects of Peripherality

Since the mid-1980s a substantial literature has been produced on the changing nature and characteristics of industrial society, in particular the increased use of new flexible production techniques, and how these changes impact on regional economic development.[6] In their seminal book, *The Second Industrial Divide*, Piore and Sabel (1984) argued that advanced industrial capitalism had reached a new stage of development which involved fundamental change. The traditional Fordist production techniques of the post-war period involved the mass production of standardised products for mass consumer markets assembled in large 'Taylorist' organised manufacturing plants. The key characteristic of this form of production was its ability to exploit economies of scale – the lowering of unit input costs as output increased. This, Piore and Sabel argue, has now given way to production based on flexible specialisation with the characteristics of small batch production, the use of advanced multi-use equipment, fragmented markets and a multi-skilled and flexible workforce. Such a paradimic shift, it is contested, has come about as the result of much increased volatility in markets during the 1970s and the development of frequently changing and more sophisticated consumer tastes and preferences. The key characteristic of flexible production is the ability to exploit economies of scope – changing the intensity and range of production, in terms of both inputs and outputs, almost instantaneously with changes in demand. This strategy of accommodating ceaseless change and encouraging permanent innovation creates an industrial environment in which competition is based on innovation and product quality, rather than the Fordist emphasis on price and stability (Best, 1990).

In terms of regional economic development it has been observed that it is those areas which have adopted flexible production techniques most fully that appear, to differing degrees and in different forms, to have achieved most success. The most common examples are Emilia Romagna in northern Italy, Baden-Wurttemberg in Germany, Jutland in Denmark, Silicon Valley in

California and Route 128 in Boston. In addition to the use of flexible specialisation, a fundamental characteristic of the economies of these different areas is the existence of strong industrial districts or clusters of interlinked activity.

The concept of industrial clusters and the spatial concentration of interdependent economic activity is by no means a new phenomenon. The economist Alfred Marshall (1920), more than seventy years ago, emphasised the benefits to be gained through external economies of scale for firms concentrating together in specific geographic areas. Indeed the inherent creation of spatial inequalities as a result of the operation of modern industrial capitalism has been the very basis of regional economics as a discipline. Myrdal (1957) discussed the concept of cumulative causation, and the idea that the economic fortunes of areas would tend to diverge rather than converge, while Perroux (1955) raised the idea of developing specific areas through a policy of growth poles. Indeed the very operation of regional policies, at both the national and European level, is based on the simple understanding that economic development takes place in a spatially uneven manner. More fundamentally, Mjoset (1992) in his far-reaching study of Ireland, draws on a wide range of economic, political, social and cultural factors, and argues that Ireland, especially the Republic, has become caught in a vicious circle of peripheral development which contrasts with the virtuous circle of autocentric development of other similar economies such as Austria, Denmark, Finland and Sweden.

Industrial clusters or districts have been seen to be at the heart of successful regional-based economies in the recent past. Porter (1990) stresses how a number of firms in vigorous competition stimulate the rapid development of skilled human resources, technologies, market specific knowledge and specialised infrastructure. Clusters embody many of the characteristics of agglomeration economies – the idea that the benefits of the whole are greater than the sum of its parts. Industries are linked through vertical (buyer/supplier) or horizontal (enterprises that have common customers, employ related technologies and use the same channels of communication) relationships. Successful clusters encourage both rival enterprises and related and supporting industries. This allows rapid interchanges of technology and market information among vertically and horizontally related enterprises meaning high degrees of cooperation. Indeed successful clusters are characterised by a strong mixture of both competition and cooperation. In essence clusters maintain diversity through avoiding inwardness, economic inertia and inflexibility all of which are structural impediments which halt sustainable economic development.

The implication for peripherality of the emergence of new industrial clusters and districts is obvious, since by definition they are concentrated in specific geographic areas. Spatial inequalities, therefore, increase according to the extent that these areas develop, while others ossify. As Scott and Storper (1990) argue, the geographic distribution of flexible production agglomerations is extremely uneven. An important question for a region such as Northern Ireland, therefore, is whether it can develop successful clusters. Flexible specialisation is very much part of the new industrial districts and in many ways has been an integral part of their successful development. One aspect, for example, is the use of Just-in-Time (J-I-T) techniques whereby firms minimise the stockholding of material inputs by having them constantly delivered to the factory for immediate use. Japanese companies are perhaps the best known exponents of such techniques. To function effectively, J-I-T, not surprisingly, requires suppliers to be located close to manufacturers and for supplies to be transported quickly on high quality infrastructure.[7] This is one way in which industrial districts can be seen to have developed.

It is fairly obvious that such systems of production mitigate against areas which are geographically distant from the core districts. In the case of Northern Ireland it would be highly unlikely for firms in the region to be able to service those more highly developed core areas because of the high transport costs and long delivery times that would be required. Moreover, the exchange of information and the development of long-term relationships between firms, that industrial districts encourage, lowers transactions costs in these core areas and this acts to their significant competitive advantage (Clulow and Teague, 1993). This is a further instance where fundamental changes in the economic circumstances of production interact with the concept of peripherality and help us to go beyond the narrow geographic concept of transport costs.

The key players in modern international capitalism are, of course, transnational corporations (TNCs) which play a substantial role in determining the relative success of regions and, in the context of this chapter, degrees of economic peripherality. In the case of industrial policy in Northern Ireland there has been a strong emphasis on the attraction of foreign investment. Such investment has largely come in the form of Fordist organised branch plants with few linkages to the rest of the economy (NIEC, 1992; Hamilton, 1993). Although not as successful in this policy approach as the Republic of Ireland, it is probably reasonable to describe Northern Ireland's industrialisation process as one based on the 'peripheralisation of Fordism'. In this respect the incentives package used to attract industry has been, and continues to be, almost wholly based on the provision of generous grants and tax subsidies. Such an approach, however, encourages the very type of economic activity that has been found inimical to successful regional economic development, at least in the context of the examples cited here. Therefore, even if Northern Ireland were as successful – in terms of gaining large numbers of foreign plants – as the Republic, such a policy of attracting Fordist-type foreign investment would, because of its ambiguity and fragility, be potentially harmful to long-term development. The other side of the coin, in terms of the role of TNCs, is that Northern Ireland has very few TNCs of its own. This means that the potential benefits in terms of research and development, management and other high value activities of TNCs that typically reside in the home economy, are absent. This contributes also to economic peripherality.

One final, but important, characteristic of the successful regions mentioned is the existence of a highly effective and virtuous governance structure (Clulow and Teague, 1993). What is meant by this, simply, is the nature of institutional frameworks within the region and whether the external environment which this creates meshes effectively with individual firms and fosters and encourages cooperation between firms. The governance structure covers the full range of institutions from universities, financial bodies and development agencies through to government itself, and needs to provide common services, encourage collective commercial action and take a long-term perspective. Moreover, the enterprise calculations which companies adopt in terms of the type of competitive strategy they follow (a stress on research and development, skill formation and new technology rather than cost minimisation) are of equal importance, especially when linked to the other strands of the governance structure. Scott and Storper conclude in this respect that 'the viability of contemporary flexible production agglomerations depends in high degree upon effective institution-building at the regional level' (1990, p. 44).

In the case of Northern Ireland, Clulow and Teague (1993) argue convincingly that every level and component of the governance structure is faulty and, therefore, a serious impediment to improved economic performance. Therefore, if effective regional economic development is to occur then the need for an improved governance structure not only has to be recognised by government in its approach to policy, but acted upon.

Current developments in international capitalism – the adoption of new production techniques and corporate strategies – the role of TNCs, and the creation of industrial districts and increased regional inequalities, have all left Northern Ireland more peripheral and without substantial changes in transport costs and infrastructure. In addition, it needs to be stressed that the violent political situation in Northern Ireland, while necessarily at the core of any analysis of the local economic situation, adds substantially to the peripheralisation of the regional economy in the wider European and global context. This is particularly so in relation to the development of an effective governance structure.

Conventional Policy Perspectives

Given that Northern Ireland is both geographically and economically peripheral and, as a result, is at a serious disadvantage in terms of improving its economic development, it is essential that new and more effective policy perspectives are brought to bear on the deep economic problems of Northern Ireland. One useful approach, as adopted in a more general context by Clulow and Teague (1993), is to examine what would be needed for Northern Ireland to become a counter core. Certainly, centres of economic activity in Europe have changed over the recent past and, therefore, it is worth considering what would be required for Northern Ireland to move upwards from its disadvantageous position in the core-periphery hierarchy.[8]

Perhaps the first point is that a fundamental change of attitudes and approach is needed on the part of both government and industry in Northern Ireland. In terms of government there is little to suggest that the successful experiences of other European regions, and the new thinking on which it is based, have filtered through to those who formulate and implement economic development policy. Indeed it could be argued that such inward-looking thinking may itself be a reflection of peripherality. Whatever the reason for this, it is imperative that the lessons from other more successful parts of Europe (and even further afield) begin to permeate policy discussion in Northern Ireland.

There have been quite significant and positive changes in policy in recent years in Northern Ireland, reflected in *Competing in the 1990s* and the subsequent strategies of the development agencies (IDB, 1990; LEDU, 1991). However, the focus on improved competitiveness as the key to economic development, while not necessarily wrong, needs to be shifted away from the needs and concerns of individual firms and relocated in the wider context of industrial clusters, flexible specialisation and the new forms of competition and cooperation touched on in this chapter. In other words the competitive strategy presented in *Competing in the 1990s* would need to become more systemic and less concerned with the needs of individual firms in isolation.[9] Such an approach would fit policy more appropriately and more effectively into the observed parameters of regional economic success experienced elsewhere. At the level of industry in Northern Ireland, it seems far from evident that flexible systems of production are commonplace (although there is admittedly little evidence), or that they have been encouraged by policy.[10] If Northern Ireland does not adapt its production techniques to those required for successful economic development, then its Fordist peripheralisation and subsequent laggard rate of development is more than likely to continue.

It is difficult to envisage any more than two core economic areas in the UK (the existing one in the southeast and the need for a new one to be created in the north). If this is so, and it seems likely, then Northern Ireland would not be an obvious location as a new core area. In this context it would, therefore, seem sensible for Northern Ireland to attempt to create some form of core economic area with the Republic of Ireland. Munck (1993) has shown that a number of substantial benefits would arise from the creation of a truly all-Ireland economy. Such benefits would include the opportunity for indigenous industry to build upon and exploit a larger home market and, therefore, economies of scale which would assist immeasurably in the ability to compete internationally (O'Malley, 1989).[11] An all-Ireland economy would also provide the ability to benefit more fully from external economies of scale through the clustering of industrial activity, and much more effective and less wasteful coordination of almost all aspects of government policy, including industrial development, health care, tourism, agriculture, energy and transport. Combined with a deep democratisation of the economy, Munck suggests that such an approach would lead to greater diversity, flexibility and creativity; factors all prevalent in the examples of successful economies discussed in this chapter. Moreover, the potential for the development of an appropriate and supportive governance structure is more likely to be achieved in an all-Ireland economy characterised by greater integration, coherence and coordination. In this context it is absolutely essential to recognise and engage with the important two-way links between the economy and Irish polity.

Conclusion

When extending this discussion and placing it within the literature of flexible specialisation and the new regionalism, it is important to stress the need for greater autonomy. As part of an economic strategy for the island of Ireland, this would emphasise the development of indigenous industry, which draws on indigenous resources and which is geared to indigenous demands and needs. If such a strategy could be fleshed out then industry in both the North and South of Ireland would be in a far stronger position to integrate into the global economy, rather than continuing its peripheralisation through its ultimately harmful dependence on foreign capital.

Part of the process of socio-economic reorganisation must begin with an examination of the recent thinking and experiences of regional economic development which are applicable to the situation in Northern Ireland in relation to the wide-ranging concept of peripherality. Central to the discussion of policy is the suggestion that the benefits of sustained regional development experienced elsewhere, in particular flexible specialisation, industrial clusters and an effective governance structure, will only have a chance of taking place in Northern Ireland if the economies in the North and South of Ireland are brought together into one coherent unit. New perspectives and ideas need to be brought to bear on the deep-rooted problems of the Northern Ireland economy, and these have to be linked with the economic and political realities of the current stage of global capitalism. If not, then it is likely that the seemingly endemic failure of the regional economy for over sixty years will not be reversed. It is in this wider and more fundamental context that the importance of economic peripherality lies.

Notes

1. Peripherality can be interpreted in a number of ways – geographic, economic, social, political, psychological and cultural. This chapter does not attempt to cover all these interpretations.
2. Fordist production systems are characterised by standard products, long production lines, vertical integration of enterprises and the ability to exploit internal economies of scale. Post-Fordist systems, on the other hand, involve flexible and multi-use equipment, small batch production, product differentiation and the ability to exploit economies of scope.
3. It is commonly agreed that the level of cross-border trade in Ireland is well below that in other similar sized neighbouring economies and that substantial scope exists for increased trade and economic activity within Ireland (Quigley, 1992). Moreover, it has been argued that the abolition of custom controls, with the creation of the single European market, has been accompanied by an increase in the militarisation of the Irish border and the closure of border roads for 'security' reasons which act against economic development.
4. Northern Ireland had a gross domestic product per head of population in 1992 only 80 per cent of that for the UK, which itself is below the EU average; less than one in five of the workforce is employed in manufacturing; and the unemployment rate at around 15 per cent is one of the highest in the EU, with over half the jobless out of work for over a year. Importantly the Northern Ireland economy is kept afloat by a subvention from Britain (the amount needed to cover the difference between public expenditure and tax revenue) which totalled around £4 billion in 1993, one third of GDP.
5. In other words there is an asymmetric relationship between the core and the periphery in that peripheral regions lose from poor transport infrastructure, but core regions gain when it is improved.
6. There remains some debate as to the extent and importance of flexible specialisation in advanced capitalist economies. For a recent critique of the flexible specialisation literature see Curry (1993).
7. It could be argued that what is important for J-I-T to work is when supplies arrive rather than how long they take in

transit. However, experience suggests that J-I-T manufacturers prefer suppliers to be geographically close.

8. O'Hearn (1993) argues pessimistically that in the case of the Republic of Ireland the possibility of upwards mobility is extremely limited in the context of increased European integration.
9. In theoretical terms, as Breathnach argues elsewhere in this book, this would be a move away from a policy based on neoclassical analysis to one which is more 'institutionally' oriented.
10. A worthwhile research project would be to see how true this assertion is.
11. Bradley and Wright (1993) also highlight the possible scale and agglomeration economies that could arise from the growth of indigenous industries as the result of a wider and more integrated home market.

3

Euro-regionalism: National Conflict and Development

JAMES ANDERSON AND JAMES GOODMAN

Regionally based politics at sub-state level are becoming more important within the EU. This is being encouraged by supranational institutions of the EU, by the logic of European integration and by more localised pressures for socio-economic development. Regional pressures are widely seen as eroding the nation state 'from below' while EU institutions and globalisation erode it 'from above' – a pincer movement with the potential to transform traditional conceptions of state sovereignty and national identity. In this chapter we question the predicted 'end of territorially based sovereignty' through investigating the robustness of suggestions that sub-state national conflicts, such as those in the Basque country, Corsica or Ireland, will be superseded in a 'Europe of the Regions'.[1]

The hopes invested in EU regionalism have been given a new salience by the reappearance of national conflict in eastern Europe. The fear that scores of ethnic and territorial disputes could proliferate has increased the symbolic and practical importance attached to the EU. Even John Major, leader of the sceptical British Conservative Party, sees it as offering an antidote to the destructive side of nationalism (*Guardian*; September 8, 1992). The development of the Single European Market (SEM) and the aspiration to monetary and political union as expressed in the 'Maastricht Treaty' have also stimulated hopes that regionalism could become a benign alternative to nation states and nationalism. Some believe that accelerated EU integration could effectively end the torment of Northern Ireland in a system of regional as opposed to national representation.

But just what 'regionalism' means in Ireland is at best disputed and sometimes it simply reflects existing positions on the national conflict. Some unionists argue for instance that the North will remain a region of the United Kingdom and that EU integration will encourage the South to discard its out-dated nationalism and accept membership of the 'British Isles'. On the other hand many Irish nationalists hope that increasing economic cooperation between North and South will lead to the political reunification of the island in a new Irish Republic. Others, however, envisage a decentralisation of power and the growth of regional and local government in the existing Irish Republic and in Northern Ireland. There are hopes that Northern Ireland will be defined as a region of the EU, rather than a region of the British or the Irish state, and that this could lead to a solution to the conflict (Anderson and Goodman, 1993). We situate these various hopes in the context of the changing roles of states and regions within the EU in general, and the United Kingdom and the Irish Republic in particular. We describe the influence of EU institutions and economic integration on the two states, contrasting their highly centralised political structures with general tendencies in the EU, and we discuss the implications of these tendencies for the national conflict. Are regional economic developments leading to a solution to the conflict, or is the conflict hampering cooperation and development?

EU Integration and Regional Assertion

In response to their individual vulnerabilities in an increasingly globalised world market, EU states have been pooling their resources and concentrating economic power at the European level. Motivated by the economic crisis of the late 1970s and by fears of heightened competition from North American and East Asian economies, member states have increasingly put their faith in action at the community level. The EU, however, remains essentially an inter-governmental organisation rooted in the established power structures of the individual states. It is dominated by the Council of Ministers representing the member states, rather than by the more fully supranational European Parliament or the European Commission. Membership of the EU gives the states greater leverage over economic forces, provides them with a new arena in which to exercise power and in some respects enhances rather than diminishes their authority (Taylor, 1983).

The state has not been superseded from above, or undermined from below, and reports of its death are distinctly premature. Rather it is in the process of adapting to increasing international contacts and to the shifting demands of sub-state elites who are themselves responding to the same globalising tendencies. A 'Europe of the regions' is not on the agenda, but growing regionalism is. Although the state remains the main political framework for social organisation, EU integration has regionalised what until recently could be described as 'national' economies and it has heightened the need for regional, as distinct from state, channels of political representation. This emerging regionalism is fostered by EU institutions, particularly the Commission and Parliament, and by forces in the regions responding to the logic of integration. However, in the first instance it is controlled by the states themselves. The individual states determine what is and what is not deemed to constitute a 'region' for EU purposes, and they control the decentralisation of formal powers to regional levels of government. Some member states have decentralised administration to regional authorities and given constitutional guarantees of regional autonomy. In some cases, for example Spain, regional powers have been granted as part of a general process of democratising state structures (Vandamme, 1981). Elected regional bodies are now an established feature of political life in four of the five largest EU states and in several of the smaller ones, and the British and Irish states stand out as major exceptions to the general rule (Council of Europe, 1988; Keating, 1988).

The European Commission and Parliament, together with the newly established Committee of the Regions and the older Council of Europe, make a direct and very significant contribution to the legitimation and mobilisation of sub-state national and regional movements. The Commission has encouraged the growth of regional representation to enhance its own powers *vis-à-vis* the state governments, as well as to improve transnational economic and social cohesion. In alliance with the regions, it has formulated an EU-wide regional development policy which focuses on regions rather than states and thus has the potential both to legitimise regional movements and undermine existing state authority. The Parliament and its Regional Policy Committee have played a central role in driving forward this Commission agenda. Regionalism is also fostered from within the regions themselves. Disputes over the regional distribution of EU funding by state governments have proliferated across the EU, and in some cases – notably in Portugal, Greece and Ireland – these disputes have stimulated demands for representative structures at regional level. The logic of integration, and particularly of the SEM, which demands more direct region-to-region contacts across state borders, has increased the significance of development strategies at sub-state regional levels, and in consequence greater regional powers are increasingly seen as essential.

Since 1979, the Commission of the European Communities' (CEC) reports on regional development have attempted to monitor how far 'national' economies are being regionalised (CEC, 1984). The *Third Report* (1987) argued that inter-regional disparities were becoming more important than inter-state disparities – inter-regional inequalities were accelerating at an alarming rate while differences between states had not widened – and in 1990, two years before the official 'completion' of the Single Market, the *Fourth Report* speculated that these disparities were being caused by the processes of integration (CEC, 1990). In 1991 the Commission's discussion document on regional development, *Europe 2000*, argued that 'new location factors' emerging from the changing structure of economic activity would help to reverse these regional disparities (CEC, 1991), but as yet there is little evidence that these factors are sufficiently powerful to counter the tendencies towards increasing regional disparities in the deregulated SEM.

The continuation, and indeed sharpening of differences between regions, is encouraging the formation of inter-regional alliances across the EU. It is generally the more prosperous and autonomous regions which have taken the lead, forging new inter-regional development axes such as the so-called 'four motors' of Catalonia, Rhone-Alpes, Baden-Wurttemburg and Lombardy; these regions of Spain, France, Germany and Italy, respectively, have formed another association of the 'haves'[2] similar to the Organisation for Economic Cooperation and Development (OECD) or the 'G7' group of the world's leading industrialised states. Individual 'peripheral' regions may bargain for an association with such alliances, but mainly they have formed their own alliances, such as the Conference of Peripheral Maritime Zones, or partnerships have begun to develop between immediately neighbouring peripheral regions such as Northern Ireland and the Irish Republic. Thus, within the EU as a whole, regionalism has become established as an increasingly important feature of politics, because of the actions of individual states and central EU institutions and the logic of the SEM. Britain and Ireland, however, present a contrasting picture.

Regionalism in Britain and Ireland

The centralised nature of the state in the UK and in the Irish Republic is a major obstacle to the full development of regionalism in Britain and Ireland, and it has been thrown into sharp relief by the demands of EU integration. Indeed both states have tended to ignore these demands, and they act as a limiting, rather than a facilitating, factor with respect both to integration and regionalism. This, as we shall see, has increasingly significant consequences for the national conflict. The UK is held together by a centralised state apparatus legitimised by the sovereignty of the Crown over its subjects (Crick, 1991). Parliament governs with some administrative powers devolved to local authorities and to appointed elites. In the 1970s proposals to democratise the British system of government were shelved, and since 1979, partly because of ideological conflicts between central government and local government, there has been a weakening of formal democratic government at local and regional levels.[3]

At the same time, however, the local state, defined as including recently established appointed bodies as well as elected councils, has retained its importance. Regionalist and nationalist movements in the UK, as elsewhere, have been reinvigorated by EU integration, EU institutions, and the uneven effects of economic recession. Accelerated industrial collapse coupled with reductions in regional development subsidies (which fell from 0.7 per cent to 0.2 per cent of UK GDP between 1975 and 1985) sharpened the unemployment disparities between UK regions, from an average gap of 2.1 per cent in the years 1959–76 to an average of 8 per cent by the late 1980s (MacKay, 1992). In response to the growth in unemployment disparities, regionalist groupings such as the Campaign for a Scottish, for a Welsh and, in England, for a Northern Assembly, have argued that regional autonomy is urgently required to prevent further peripheralisation in the Single Market. Fearing further deterioration and hoping for greater development opportunities within the EU framework, UK regional interests and perceptions are being transformed. This is true of regions in England but it is particularly the case in Scotland, Wales and Northern Ireland which already have first hand experience of peripherality within the UK and have developed political cultures which are very distinct from the dominant English southeast.

Regionalist groupings and nationalist parties at sub-state level have, therefore, generally welcomed integration in the EU, in sharp contrast to British nationalists and the representatives of the central state who fear that EU integration may fragment the UK. Regionally based groups and institutions have increasingly made links with similar or adjacent regions elsewhere in the EU – for instance Kent has joined with Nord-Pas de Calais in northern France and three provinces of Belgium to form the Transmanche 'Euro region' (Balsom, 1990; Brand, 1990; Cochrane, 1993).[4] Regionalist and nationalist campaigners now frame their demands in explicitly European terms: the Scottish National Party manifesto for the 1992 General Election called for Scottish independence to maximise the opportunities for Scotland in Europe: the Welsh Plaid Cymru similarly called for 'full self government ... within the EC'.[5] This redefinition of regional and 'national' regional interests within the UK has been actively encouraged by EU institutions. The Commission, for instance, has stressed regional as against state interests in the distribution of Structural Funds; it has become a useful ally of UK regions which attempt to challenge the development priorities of Westminster and Whitehall; and many regions have opened offices in Brussels to strengthen their direct links with EU institutions and other regions.[6] EU integration is highlighting what many see as an anachronistic overcentralisation of the state and politics in the UK.

State centralism in the Irish Republic has different causes and circumstances but its effects may be similar. The state has a population of 3.5 million, about a third of which is concentrated in the capital, Dublin. In size it contrasts with the UK's population of 56.4 million, and is considerably smaller than the population of such EU regions as Lombardy and Catalonia. While the British state was built on conquest, the Republic was built on an anti-colonial struggle against it, though the Republic's overcentralisation is seen by some as part of the colonial legacy. Whereas the UK is internally divided into a number of distinct regional and national groupings, the Republic is relatively homogeneous culturally and politically. Fear of fragmentation is therefore not a factor in the Republic as it is in the UK. Instead, state centralism is maintained by a political culture of 'clientelism' in which parliamentary representatives operate by obtaining, or appearing to obtain, political leverage for their localities at the centre. As a result, the political elite either fails to see state centralism as a problem or has a vested interest in its continuation, or both.[7]

Thus, like the UK, but perhaps with more reason given its smaller size and greater homogeneity, the Republic has 'opted out' of the EU-wide tendency to devolve power to sub-state levels. It has no elected regional authorities; local government is largely conducted through County Councils whose chief executives are appointed by central government; and the Councils' limited financial and political powers have been further whittled away in recent years.[8] As in the UK, political debate on the Republic's lack of regional government has been encouraged by the Commission and Parliament. In 1987 the Parliament highlighted the issue,[9] and in 1988 the Dublin government was forced to re-establish regional advisory bodies to oversee the distribution of European funds just one year after regional bodies had been dissolved as part of a budget cut! Following continuing criticisms, the Commission President held direct consultations with Irish government ministers. In 1990 the *Barrington Report* by an Irish Commission of Enquiry into Local Government compared the Republic with other European states and concluded that it 'lagged behind with overly centralised institutions of government' (Dublin Stationery Office, 1990, p. 19), but its recommendations have not been acted on.[10] Over-centralisation both in the Republic and in Northern Ireland has significantly hampered cross-border cooperation.

Cooperation has also been hampered by divergences in the stances of the two governments towards the EU. For example, politicians in the Republic have tried to define their economy as part of the EU 'core', or, as the then Taoiseach Charles Haughey put it, 'safe in the middle of the pack' (*Guardian*, February 8, 1992). Following the collapse of Sterling and its departure from the Exchange Rate Mechanism (ERM) in October 1992, the Irish government was determined to maintain the value of the Punt within the ERM (*Irish Times*, February 12, 1993). In contrast to the British, the Irish political establishment aspired to membership of the Germany-led 'fast lane' of European monetary union.[11] Indeed this aspiration was partly motivated by a desire to further reduce over-dependency on markets in a declining British economy, as well as reflecting a reluctance to be labelled a 'peripheral' economy. One result has been a lack of joint working with other peripheral EU regions, including Northern Ireland, though this may be due to inter-regional competition for trans-national inward investment.[12]

The aspiration to be in the 'fast lane' revealed the lack of priority given to cross-border cooperation. Had it been realised, it would have made inter-regional cooperation with the North even more difficult, as Northern Ireland, along with the rest of the UK, languished in the 'slow lane'. However, in the event it failed. Despite Irish government interventions to defend its currency, speculation eventually forced a devaluation, back into closer parity with Sterling. An altogether chastening experience with government ministers expressing 'deep disillusionment with the failure of EC solidarity' (*Financial Times*, October 6, 1992). This failure reflected the relatively minor importance of the Punt in the ERM and the fact that the Republic's economy was still tied to the UK. It confirmed its peripheral status in the emerging EU. The other side of the coin is that North–South cooperation has become both more feasible and more necessary. Integration into the SEM, and increasing concerns at dependence on transnational branch plants, their lack of local linkages and their propensity to closure, have highlighted the need to maximise Ireland's indigenous economic potential (Munck, 1993). Such a reorientation of economic development strategy would make North–South linkages and the achieving of an integrated 'one island economy' a higher priority.

Regionalism and the National Conflict

The SEM is threatening increased competition from stronger economies and a further centralisation of economic wealth within the EU. This is heightening perceptions, locally and in Brussels, that if the two parts of Ireland don't 'swim together' they may 'sink separately'. Perhaps the single most important structural change bearing on the conflict is the fact that Irish business leaders, and particularly Northern ones, have taken the initiative on North–South economic integration as an end in itself. This has had the unintended effect of renewing hopes that the economic integration of the two regions in an EU context will lead to the Irish nationalist goal of political reunification. On the other hand, the on-going conflict and paramilitary activity by Loyalists and Republicans constitute a major obstacle to economic integration, and in any case economic developments will not on their own solve the political conflict. On the contrary, the lack of an adequate political programme and framework is perhaps the biggest obstacle to achieving economic integration (Anderson and Shuttleworth, 1992–3; Anderson, 1994). It is clear that the comparatively weak regionalism of Britain and Ireland will not solve the conflict. But equally, the ways in which the conflict is conducted and managed, and in which solutions are sought, will increasingly be influenced by European integration and regionalism. In assessing the interrelationships between regionalism and the conflict, we need to consider the role of EU institutions and the business pressures for North–South integration, and we must also take account of the obstacles to integration.

Both the European Parliament and the Commission have seen the conflict as undermining European ideals. In 1983 for instance Commission officials were describing it as a 'blot on the community'.[13] From its first session, the Parliament has questioned British policy in the North and since 1981 it has passed several resolutions critical of the British government. Northern Ireland was identified as one of the most serious problems facing the EU (European Parliament, 1984); and in response to pressure from the Parliament, Commission officials in the mid-1980s argued that EU involvement would offer a much better hope of a long-term solution. Irish Members of the European Parliament raised the issue of Ireland's economic integration and called on the Commission to distribute funds on an all-Ireland basis. Since 1982 Commissioners have highlighted the need for the North and South of Ireland to act together at the EU level, to recognise the problems which are common to both regions, and to draw up joint plans for dealing with them. Since 1991 the Commission has openly advocated the need for joint North–South institutions to facilitate closer economic integration and to address the political issues involved; and in 1993 it proposed that there should be a specific North–South component to the Structural Funds for the two regions.

These various proposals reflect the growing similarity of North and South in terms of the structure of their economies and their economic problems. This historical trend has accelerated since both entered the 'Common Market' in 1973, and there are now larger economic differences between Northern Ireland and the rest of the UK. Despite, or perhaps because of, its increased dependence on the financial subvention from the British Exchequer, the North's economy is in some respects increasingly detached from the economy of Britain. For instance it was barely touched by the British credit boom of the mid-1980s (Hart and Harrison, 1992). This, along with fears of peripheralisation in the SEM, is the context which explains the new enthusiasm for North–South cooperation in business circles. It is widely anticipated that Ireland, North and South, will become a 'one island economy' as advocated by the Chairman of the Ulster Bank, Dr George Quigley (1992). The Northern Ireland Chamber of Commerce has taken practical initiatives to improve links with the South,[14] and the regional branch of the Confederation of British Industry has begun working jointly with its Southern counterpart, the Irish Business and Employers Confederation, to further inter-regional partnership. They have lobbied the Commission for EU funds to support North–South economic integration, which in turn encourages and gives legitimacy to the pressures from EU institutions.[15]

These pressures 'from above and below' make a 'compelling' case for closer North–South cooperation, and it has received at least formal backing from both governments. In October 1992 the British Secretary of State for Northern Ireland stated that the British government wished to improve North–South cooperation; and in the same year the Irish government published an in-depth investigation of the implications of EU integration which concluded that 'the costs of the current one island/two economy basis of operation in many areas will become a greater drag on economic progress' (Dublin Stationery Office, 1992a, p. 32). This will be even more the case if North and South do reorientate their economic development strategies towards more indigenous and integrated growth, as distinct from aiming to provide 'export platforms' for transnational branch plants. The similar problems and needs of two low-income peripheral economies with weak indigenous development are increasingly being recognised (Dublin Stationery Office, 1992b). As EU integration proceeds, integrated North–South development in Ireland is likely to become a more urgent political issue.

Given that the national conflict is about the political unification or separation of North and South, these economic developments are bound to have implications for it. But a number of qualifications must be considered. There are serious obstacles to economic integration. Its pace and depth are reduced by political factors and, in particular, by the conflict. Moreover, the effects of economic integration on the conflict are mostly indirect or tangential. At one level, integration is very directly hampered by the military conflict, by for example the fortification of the border and political violence against North–South economic infrastructure such as rail and electricity links. At another level, unionists, like British nationalists more generally, but in contrast to Scottish, Welsh and Irish nationalists, are hostile to any implication that European integration might weaken the regional cohesion of the UK and alter its territorial make-up. Nationalist enthusiasm for the EU feeds unionist suspicions, though unionists have been forced to acknowledge the economic logic of cooperation with the South. Where previously they rejected economic links as inevitably leading to political ones, they now argue for a sharp separation between 'economics' and 'politics', and this has helped to block the development of a political and institutional framework for establishing stronger economic links (Anderson and Goodman, 1994).

Economic progress is intertwined with political progress – or the lack of it. Economic integration requires political initiatives, particularly the establishment of North–South economic institutions, but these have become 'bargaining chips' in the inter-party talks and therefore dependent on wider agreement on constitutional issues. The result, over two years after Dr Quigley and his business associates called for a 'one island economy', is that the formal support from both governments has not, so far, been translated into substantive initiatives. The governments have been under considerable pressure from EU institutions, as we have seen, but these institutions are politically and economically circumscribed. European pressure and the emergence of an 'EC engendered trust' between the Irish and British governments were instrumental in them agreeing to establish the Anglo-Irish Inter-Governmental Conference on the North in 1985; and the Conference provides the beginnings of a framework for economic integration. But, paradoxically, this Anglo-Irish agreement has shielded both governments from further external pressures; and in any event the powers of central EU institutions are strictly limited as the EU remains a state-dominated organisation. Their powers are also economically circumscribed by the smallness of the EU budget, and in the case of Northern Ireland the regional subsidies from the EU are dwarfed by dependency on the British subvention. This dependency is a measure of the North's economic plight and, while it does not rule out integration with the South, as unionists now like to claim, it points both to the EU's financial limitations and the North's continuing need for external aid from whatever sources.[16]

The reciprocal effects of economic integration in mitigating the conflict are also limited, and not just because integration is still weakly developed. While the conflict centrally involves North–South relations, it also involves sectarian relations within Northern Ireland. The two issues are closely interrelated but economic cooperation between North and South cannot of itself cure sectarianism in the North. Many unionist business people may have changed their attitudes to the South, but the mainly working-class unionist and nationalist communities which support the various paramilitaries are perhaps the last to be influenced by EU-related developments and rhetoric. For them the SEM may mean simply the threat of even higher unemployment. More generally, the impact of EU developments is limited by some of the political effects of the conflict such as the extreme weakness of local government, the unaccountability of the Northern Ireland Office, the 'political vacuum' in the North, and the priority ascribed to security policy. Since 1982, and ostensibly for security reasons, Commission funding initiatives on the border have been centrally controlled at inter-governmental level by the two states, in breach of EU funding regulations and contrary to the expressed wishes of the European Parliament.[17]

Overall, a curious dualism has emerged as the two governments strive to contain the political and military conflict in the North, while at the same time attempting, however inadequately, to increase economic integration. In 1988, for instance, Irish and British ministers were discussing cross-border cooperation at a conference near Brussels while the two governments were politically at loggerheads over an extradition case (Fenn, 1989). This dualism and the contradictory relations arising from it are perhaps sharpest in border areas: on the one hand EU integration undermines the significance of the border and there are expectations that it will remove partition; on the other hand the border has been further fortified.[18]

Conclusion

EU integration and regional economic developments have so far had only a limited effect on the national conflict. But they point towards solutions which involve greater economic and political integration of Ireland's two regions, whether in a unitary or a federal structure, or, perhaps more likely in the short term, with some elements of 'shared sovereignty' involving both the British and the Irish states.[19]

Globalisation and European integration are altering the role of nation states but not in ways which would make nationalisms and national conflict historically redundant. The EU has played a key role in accelerating a 'decay of that older relationship between national capitalism and national solidarity' (*Guardian*, January 28, 1993), but the inter-governmentalism of the EU has mainly been a means of preserving and in some respects enhancing state power. The 'end of territorially based sovereignty' is not in sight, a 'Europe of the Regions' remains wishful thinking, and in Ireland the national conflict continues to hamper inter-regional cooperation. The suggestion that such conflicts will be superseded by regionalism has little basis in reality for the foreseeable future.

But realism about such overblown prognostications should not blind us to the increasing influence of regionalism and its growing impact on the conflict. The logic of the Single Market and the activities of EU institutions, including the new Committee of the Regions, are pushing even the highly centralised British and Irish states closer towards the continental norm of regionalisation. Regional interests are being stimulated and redefined in a more globalised and 'Europeanised' political economy, and this is sharpening the tensions between the 'national' politics of states and the regionalist politics of some EU institutions and regional authorities. In Ireland these tensions are mainly expressed through the national conflict and the political implications of an emerging 'all-Ireland' economy. A key issue is the establishment of joint North–South institutions and the powers they need to be given in order to make economic integration a reality. This issue is of central importance for the political, as well as economic, future of the island.

Notes

1. This chapter is mainly based on official documents and on Irish and British newspaper sources (see notes, below) to reflect public policies and public debates around European integration and the conflict. It is part of a larger research project and many of the arguments covered here have been discussed in interviews with leading political and economic representatives in Northern Ireland and with officials and politicians in Brussels (Anderson and Goodman, 1994).
2. The section of the chapter benefited from comments when presented in a different version at the conference on *Economic Change and Development: Prospects for Peripheral Regions*, held at Queen's University Belfast in September 1993 under the auspices of the European Society for Irish Studies, the Regional Studies Association and the ESRC.
3. The recommendation that England should be administered by five provincial councils was not implemented in the 1972 Local Government Act. The ideological conflict between central government and regional, metropolitan or local government has subsequently been reflected in the transfer of administrative powers from the latter to centrally appointed quangos or to Whitehall (Gordon, 1990); in central government dissolving the metropolitan authorities in 1984; and, more recently, in threats to dissolve regional and county

authorities in 1993 (see Hayton, 1992; ACC, 1992; *Municipal Journal*, February 19, 1993).

4. The *Planner*, November 27, 1992, and *Financial Times*, June 18, 1993.
5. *Telegraph*, March 30, 1992. The SNP argued that the Scottish people faced a 'choice to go forward with the mainstream of Europe or be stuck in a backwater of Britain': *Independent*, March 16, 1992). Plaid Cymru have welcomed EU integration and condemned the British Conservative Party as 'obsessed with the sovereignty of the UK': *Telegraph*, March 20, 1992, and *Guardian*, March 30, 1992).
6. *Guardian*, February 27, 1992 and March 2, 1992. In March 1993, twenty four representations had been established by UK local government and regional consortia in Brussels: *Telegraph*, March 5, 1993.
7. In 1990 Taoiseach Charles Haughey argued that the EC-wide tendency to devolve power to subnational regions would have little impact in the Republic, centralism was not a political issue and he anticipated that the present structures would 'broadly be kept in place, though perhaps beginning to operate in different ways and through different procedures': *Irish Times*, May 12, 1990).
8. In 1988 local authority expenditure stood at 4.2 per cent of Irish GNP: *Irish Times*, November 11, 1988. Local powers have been reduced. For example, the national Roads Authority took over responsibility for major roads in 1988; agricultural matters came under the new Agriculture and Food Development Authority; and in 1992 responsibility for the protection of the environment was handed over to another state-wide agency.
9. In 1987 the European Parliament adopted a report which highlighted the centralised structure of the Irish state and the need for regional bodies to 'promote their region nationally and internationally and stimulate the fullest use of the region's indigenous resources'.
10. The coalition government of Fianna Fail and the Progressive Democrats could not agree on their implementation, and the 1991 District Council elections were postponed pending resolution of the government's internal political differences. The Fianna Fail–Labour coalition which took office in 1993 committed itself to examining the recommendations and to calling district elections at the same time as the European elections in June 1994: *Irish Times*, February 15, 1993.

11. *Irish Times*, February 11, 1993 and February 12, 1993. This strategy was outlined by Peter Sutherland, Chair of the Allied Irish Bank and former EC commissioner, in the *Irish Times*, January 30, 1993 and February 16, 1993.
12. In the South transnational capital accounts for over 40 per cent of manufacturing employment and the need to attract overseas capital dominates the Industrial Development Authority's strategy, despite a drastic reduction in the volume of inward capital flows in the late 1980s.
13. In the words of Commission Vice President Christopher Tugendhat in a speech on January 25, 1983, at Queen's University Belfast on the tenth anniversary of British and Irish membership of the Community.
14. *Belfast Newsletter*, February 9, 1993; the CBI's *CBINI News*, June 1992 'A Positive Approach to the New Europe'.
15. The CBI's *Priorities for European Structural Funding 1994–1998*, Chapter five 'A Joint North–South Approach', Belfast, October 8, 1992, written with the Confederation of Irish Industries in Dublin; *Euro Link*, newsletter of the Northern Ireland Centre in Europe, October 10, 1992.
16. Over a third of Northern Ireland's GDP is accounted for by the British subvention which has escalated four-fold over the last two decades to around £4 billion per year, largely to compensate for the erosion of the North's industrial base and to cover the security costs of the conflict. Unionists claim that Ireland's reunification is 'impossible' because the South could not afford to take over responsibility for the subvention. However, this argument ignores a number of factors including the potential 'peace dividend'; the economic benefits of integration; the corrosive effects of increasing dependency on large subsidies; and the improbability of Britain achieving a settlement without a guarantee to subsidise post-conflict reconstruction.
17. European Parliament 1992, *Belfast Telegraph*, July 31, 1990, and *Belfast Newsletter*, February 1, 1992.
18. *Irish Times*, October 22, 1988, and *Financial Times*, October 26, 1991.
19. *Independent*, January 28, 1993, and *Irish News*, February 19, 1993. Brendan O'Leary argued in November 1992 that 'in Western Europe "pooling sovereignty" through the EC is one way in which the sometimes conflicting interests of nations and states can be reconciled or transcended.

4

EC Structural Funds and Economic Development in the Republic of Ireland

JAMES WALSH

Economic development in Ireland since 1989 has been significantly influenced by the availability of European Community structural funds. The aim of the government in relation to the use of these funds is that they will be used to: 'achieve improved competitiveness and efficiency by tackling the problems arising from our physical peripherality within the Community, inadequate infrastructure and low population density' (Government Information Services, 1989, p. 3).

A number of assessments of the use of Structural Funds in Ireland between 1989 and 1993 have been published. A major macro-economic evaluation was commissioned by the Department of Finance, a summary of which has been published (ESRI, 1993). This report questioned the economic validity of some of the measures adopted under the current round of EC-directed fund allocations. Other studies have suggested that the Structural Funds have contributed to a deterioration in the quality of life and the depletion of natural and cultural assets, and are not sustainable in the long term (Community Workers Cooperative, 1992; Meldon, 1992). This chapter reviews the regional impact of the first round of Structural Funds in the Republic of Ireland. It will also consider the preparation process for the second round of structural and cohesion funds and examine the extent to which regional concerns are reflected in the National Development Plan for the period 1994–9.

Definition and Objectives of the Structural Funds

The Structural Funds consist of the European Regional Development Fund, the European Social Fund and the Guidance part of the Agricultural Fund. Until 1989 they were operated independently which resulted in a low level of coordination. Following the adoption of the Single European Act the size of the funds was doubled and new principles were drawn up for their operation. These included the adoption of key objectives and a strategic approach to implementation. Five objectives were identified and included:

1. To promote development and adjustment of regions whose development is lagging behind
2. To convert regions seriously affected by industrial decline
3. To combat long-term unemployment
4. To facilitate the occupational integration of young people
5. To assist the reform of the Common Agricultural Policy by
   (a) adapting production, processing and marketing structures in agriculture and forestry
   (b) promoting the development of rural areas.

The strategy proposed to achieve these objectives involves the adoption of a new approach to the utilisation of the funds. To begin with, expenditure must be concentrated on the objectives (especially objective 1) and on more carefully selected geographical areas. Ireland benefits from this change as it is classified as an 'Objective 1' region. The second principle involves coordination of the planning approach. The aim of this approach is to support measures, whether at EU, national or regional level, which can be coordinated in order to ensure a coherent approach to alleviating regional disparities. It is also envisaged that multi-annual and integrated programmes will replace single projects as the principal means of assisting regional development.

Partnership has been identified as the most important principle. In the 'Framework Regulation' for funds, partnership is defined as a process involving 'close consultation between the Commission, the Member States concerned and the competent authorities designated by the latter at national, regional, local or other level, with each party acting in pursuit of a common goal' (Commission of the European Community, 1989, p. 15). According to the same report, partnership also covers 'the preparation, financing, monitoring and assessment of operations' (Commission of the European Community, 1989, p. 19). In order for the partnership principle to work there must be a commitment to the principle of subsidiarity, which requires that decisions by governments and other agencies of public service should be taken at the lowest level possible (e.g. by local or regional authorities), and only at higher levels (central government or the Community) if there is good reason for doing so. Finally, it is envisaged that there will be on-going evaluation of the support provided from the Structural Funds in order to ensure that the funds are being used in the most efficient way.

The National Development Plan 1989–93

The Republic of Ireland has in its entirety been identified as an 'Objective 1' region, where the principal purpose of the Structural Funds is to promote economic development. This, it is argued, is achieved through an economic strategy aimed at addressing the structural weakness in the economy and creating conditions conducive to productive investment. The fundamental objective of the National Development Plan was to advance the national and EC-wide aspiration towards greater economic and social cohesion. In order to achieve this aspiration it sought to:

1. Prepare the economy to compete successfully in the internal market after 1992
2. Stimulate the growth needed to reduce unemployment, to raise productivity and to begin to increase per capital income towards the average Community levels
3. Improve further the state of the public finances
4. Accompany economic growth with a greater social dimension
5. Protect and enhance the environment and natural resources.

The promotion of regional development within Ireland was not included as a major objective. It is only mentioned in the section dealing with industry and even in that case no specific regional measures were identified. While other sectors such as agriculture, tourism, forestry, transport and telecommunications have implications for where development activities are likely to occur, their potential contribution to reducing regional disparities within Ireland is not given any explicit recognition.

The Community Support Framework

The official agreement between the European Commission and the Irish government on the amount and form of EU assistance for the National Development Plan takes the form of a Community

Support Framework (CSF), which was finalised towards the end of 1989.[1] The legal basis for the drawdown of assistance under the CSF is provided for by twelve operational programmes. Each programme has been drawn up by the relevant government department or official agency. For example, Bord Failte, the Irish National Tourist Board, helped to put together the Tourism Operational Programme.

Data on expenditure patterns under the current CSF have been made available by the Department of Finance (1992). The data are organised according to priorities, operational programmes and sub-programmes. The analysis in the remainder of this section is based on actual expenditures in 1989, 1990 and 1991, together with forecasts for 1992 and 1993. The total structural expenditure between 1989 and 1993 is estimated to be about £9.5 billion. Of this total, almost £860 million is to be spent on energy and telecommunications projects that are part of the National Development Plan but beyond the scope of the CSF. The total actual and projected CSF-related structural expenditure amounts to £8640 million.

The allocation of funds between the four CSF priorities and the operational programmes is set out in Table 4.1. The largest share is allocated to industry and services, followed by physical infrastructure (measures to offset effects of peripherality, plus sanitary services). Taken together industry and infrastructure account for 50–55 per cent of the total expenditure. Expenditure on improving the quality of human resources occurs under three priorities and altogether amounts to about 30 per cent of the total. Unfortunately, only 18 per cent (£46m) of the total allocated to human resources (£2602m) is assigned to the programme dealing with the long-term unemployed. Other notable features of the table are the very small amounts allocated to tourism, rural development, forestry and environmentally friendly farming.

Table 4.2 summarises the total CSF-related structural expenditure in each region according to each priority. The single largest item is the expenditure on industry and services in Dublin. When the Midlands/East sub-region is combined with Dublin they account for 44 per cent of the total expenditure on industry and services. Just over half of the total investment in measures to offset the effects of peripherality also took place in these sub-regions, compared with less than 14 per cent of the total in the West and Northwest. By contrast, in the latter sub-regions expenditure on measures related to priority 1 (mainly for the rural economy) accounts for over 40 per cent of the total compared with only 7 per cent in Dublin.

Table 4.1 Total Structural Expenditure under the Community Support Framework (1989–93)

Priority	*Programme/ Subprogramme*	*Cost (£Ms)*	*% Share*
1. Agriculture, Fisheries,	Env. friendly farming	200.909	2.3
Tourism and	Forestry	213.696	2.5
Rural Development	Rural development	177.133	2.1
	Western package	138.878	1.6
	Objective 5(a) measures	850.140	9.8
	Tourism	336.172	3.9
(26.7%)	Sanitary services	388.991	4.5
2. Industry and Services	Industry and Services		
	– Development measures	2339.267	27.0
	– Human resources	868.52	10.1
(37.4%)	– VALOREN	326.003	0.3
3. Peripherality	Roads, rail, access facilities		
	STAR	1437.991	16.6
(17.4%)		66.096	0.8
4. Human Resources	Exceptional measures	932.212	10.8
	Occupational integration of disabled	258.997	3.0
	Training and trainers	121.651	1.4
	Long-term unemployed	45.814	0.5
	Occupational integration of young	237.648	2.8
(18.5%)			
TOTAL (100.0%)		8640.121	100.0

Source: Department of Finance, Community Support Framework and National Development Plan 1989–1993: Breakdown of structural spending, edition no. 4, 1992.

The main contrast between sub-regions in relation to expenditure is the overwhelming importance given to supporting the productive sectors (priorities 1 and 2) in the west and northwest compared with enabling expenditure (priorities 3 and 4) especially in Dublin, Midlands/East and Southwest. The variation in expenditure between regions is partly related to differences in the population totals. However, one should not expect the distribution of funds to be proportional to the population distribution since the per capita costs of providing a dispersed population with infrastructure, training programmes, etc. is inevitably higher. Table 4.2 summarises the per capita expenditure on each priority and the total in each region. The overall pattern displays a significant contrast between the east and west with the per capita expenditure in the Northwest almost 40 per cent in excess of the average for all regions. By contrast the figure for Dublin is about 19 per cent below the average.

Table 4.2 Distribution of Total Structural Expenditure by Priority and Sub-region (1989–93) (£Ms)[2]

Region	*Priority 1*	*Priority 2*	*Priority 3*	*Priority 4*	*Total*
Dublin	142.296	945.592	457.513	503.995	2049.396
Southeast	259.325	321.712	144.258	167.961	893.256
Southwest	322.082	404.475	238.437	205.358	1170.352
Midwest	316.871	374.619	142.541	179.347	1013.379
West	493.583	327.112	102.393	165.707	1088.795
Northwest	437.388	382.412	106.795	133.545	1060.140
Midlands/ East	334.374	475.871	312.148	240.409	1362.802
TOTAL	2305.374	3233.793	1504.087	1596.322	8640.802

Source: Department of Finance, Community Support Framework and National Development Plan 1989–1993: Breakdown of structural spending, edition no. 4, 1992.

Assessment of Impact of Structural Expenditure

It is extremely difficult at this stage to assess the impact of the current round of structural expenditure for a number of reasons. For example, it is clear that many of the adjustments taking place in each region are due to macro level events unrelated to the CSF. Changes in competition policy, new technologies, and restructuring processes all have significant locational impacts, and because of this the benefits from much of the expenditure are only likely to become evident over the medium to long term (e.g. infrastructural investment, some of the human resources investment). Moreover, even where some impacts might be expected there are serious measurement problems which are compounded by the unavailability of appropriate data. As such, the method of implementation of the CSF is quite unwieldy. There are twenty-eight separate programmes/sub-programmes which in turn are disaggregated into over one hundred measures requiring over fifty implementing agencies. This type of organisational structure does not lend itself easily to integration and coordination and it makes it difficult to devise a methodology to assess the overall coherence of the CSF.

Despite these difficulties a mid-term assessment of the impact of the CSF on each of the sub-regions, except Dublin, was undertaken in 1992.

While many worthwhile projects have been undertaken there have also been a number of deficiencies in the way in which the funds have been used.

The review for the Midlands/East region noted that there had been improvements to the communications networks, protection of the environment, especially water quality, and more effective use of the resource base, especially in relation to tourism and rural development. However, it was less confident about the outcomes in relation to the industry and services programme which it regarded as critical to the overall development of the sub-regional economy. While there had been considerable progress in attracting knowledge-based industry, there was disappointment in relation to internationally traded services and also in relation to the level of support provided to small domestic businesses. The evaluation of the impact of the tourism programme in the region revealed contrasting location patterns for private and public sector investments. There was a tendency for private sector projects to be located in close proximity to Dublin where the potential for commercial success was greatest and a tendency for the more distant locations to rely on public sector projects.

In the Midwest it was found that the private sector response in tourism was lower than expected, and also that there was insufficient attention to training and marketing which is essential if the extra capacity that has been grant aided is to be fully utilised. Little evidence of additionality in expenditure over and above the levels that prevailed in 1988 was claimed in the reviews for the west, northwest and midwest. Some of the reviews claimed that there was no indication that as yet the CSF funds were helping to reduce the disparities between Ireland and the rest of the EU and also those which exist within Ireland. The midlands/east review was also critical of the lack of support for locally based 'bottom-up' type integrated initiatives. It also claimed that there was a question mark over the long-term sustainability of the present pattern of development in the region.

The importance of partnership arrangements for the implementation of the funds was emphasised in the Framework

Regulation. The partnership experiment has involved the establishment of sub-regional review committees. These committees consist of representatives of the elected members of the local authorities in the sub-region, the county managers, representatives of the social partners, relevant government departments, and the European Commission. They do not include any representatives of the voluntary community and environmental sectors. Also omitted are representatives of state agencies that are organised on a regional basis and who are also involved in the implementation of some of the programmes. The role of the sub-committees is to receive and consider progress reports and financial statements on current and planned implementation of measures in, or significantly affecting, the sub-region concerned. While there appears to be some level of satisfaction among officials from the EU and the government departments with this arrangement, the representatives from within the regions are less sanguine. In fact they claim to be powerless and to have little influence over the way in which measures are either managed or implemented (Walsh, 1993). In essence, these groups are committees rather than partnerships.

Structural and Cohesion Funds 1994–9

The next round of Structural Funds will cover the remainder of this decade. The context within which the planning process is taking place is different in many respects from the situation in 1989, when the first National Development Plan was prepared. In the meantime the 'Maastricht Treaty' has been negotiated. It includes among its provisions a further enlargement of the Structural Funds and the establishment of a special Cohesion Fund for the four poorest member states.

A second major change has been the reform of the Common Agricultural Policy (CAP) which was concluded in 1992. There will be a significant reduction in the share of the EU budget allocated to the CAP, from 53 per cent in 1993 to 45 per cent in 1999. While in overall terms there may be some small increase in income for the majority of farmers, there will be an increasing reliance on compensation measures and the existing headage payments. This arrangement is unlikely to prove attractive to young farmers in the future and, consequently, it is likely that the size of the farming population will continue to decline. Strategies will be required to take account of the changes in the rural economy and the need to provide alternative sources of employment. A third important change since 1988 is the adoption of the concept of environmentally sustainable development by the European Council of Ministers. This has expanded in the 'Maastricht Treaty' which includes as an objective the need to promote economic and social development which is sustainable.

Apart from the changing external circumstances, the context for preparing the next National Development Plan has also been altered by the experience gained from the last CSF, along with a number of other developments. These include, probably most dramatically, a significant increase in unemployment and a high level of frustration among some groups that their particular problems, or those of their area/region, were not adequately addressed under the last CSF. Moreover, since the commencement of the last CSF there have been major reviews of local government structures and of industrial policy. The current Programme for Government contains a commitment to implement many of the recommendations from these reviews. New regional authorities were established on January 1, 1994.

Preparation of the Second National Development Plan 1994–9

The preparation of the second National Development Plan commenced early in 1992. Overall responsibility for the plan remained with the Department of Finance. A welcome aspect of the preparation was an extensive process of consultation. Detailed submissions were prepared for each of the sub-regions. There are a number of new emphases in the development objectives set out in the submissions. Each of the submissions gave high priority to employment retention and creation. This is not surprising given the scale of unemployment and the experience under the first CSF, where in most regions new employment creation was totally offset by losses of jobs that existed at the beginning of the period. The labour market situation in Dublin has deteriorated to the point where it now has the second highest unemployment rate after the northwest.

A second innovation is a strong emphasis on local development. It is envisaged that a programme for local development would not only support economic development but also facilitate a greater degree of decentralisation of decision-making and implementation. The submission from the West sub-region recommended that a local development programme should contain a strong commitment to an animation process provided by skilled community and economic development staff.

While an increased emphasis on 'bottom-up' initiatives will be generally welcomed there are a number of issues that will require further consideration before a programme on local development can be launched. These include: coordination between programmes and implementing agencies at local and national levels, provision of local infrastructural support, careful scrutiny of the viability of projects, ensuring that proper management and financial skills are in place and that there is a transparent system of accountability, avoidance of duplication of, or unfair competition between, both structures and projects. There must also be a more realistic assessment of how much can be expected from 'bottom-up' initiatives.

A further change of emphasis between the submissions and the current CSF relates to the provision of transport infrastructure. Under the first programme, to offset the effects of peripherality, the emphasis is mainly on the national roads and especially those leading into Dublin. There is a perception in the west and northwest that the levels of peripherality in those regions were not adequately addressed. This is reflected in their submissions which emphasise the need for an upgrading of the quality of the main roads. An interesting, if somewhat radical, proposal in this area is for the provision of a 'Euro-route' extending from Letterkenny to Limerick and on to Rosslare via Waterford, with branch routes to Cork and Tralee and links to the population centres of the sub-regions. This routeway would be multi-modal (road/rail/airport/seaport) and link with radial road and rail connections to Dublin. It is envisaged that the proposed routeway would significantly improve links between the sub-regions and stimulate inter-regional development. In order for this to happen, however, there should also be more detailed consideration given to the role of cities such as Cork, Limerick and Galway within the national urban system. The need to give consideration to this issue is noted in the submissions from the southwest and midwest.

Furthermore, in relation to transport infrastructure there is a widespread consensus that more resources must be allocated to the maintenance of secondary and county roads. These are very important for many small businesses located in small towns or rural areas, and also for tourism. Most of the submissions also refer to the desirability of upgrading the rail network. A reallocation of more investment towards public transport could be justified on grounds of social equity and environmental sustainability.

In contrast to the new emphases noted above, there are some areas where the amount of change has been disappointing. Processes of social exclusion and economic marginalisation are very poorly considered in most of the submissions. Additionally, the issue of sustainability is treated explicitly in only two of the regional submissions. However, at a sectoral level the draft development plan prepared by Bord Failte places quite a strong emphasis on sustainability. It claims that 'the success of our tourism plan requires a national commitment to sustainable development of every sector of the economy' (Bord Failte, 1992, p. 12). Sustainable tourism development is defined as 'a development policy which leaves the environment undiminished and, ideally, enhanced as a future tourism resource' (Bord Failte, 1992, p. 16). This emphasis on sustainability in the tourism plan is particularly important given its significance for regional development. A further weakness in most of the submissions is an almost total absence of any explicit reference to the internal diversity of the sub-regions. Both the northwest and southeast submissions refer to the need for balanced development between counties and between urban and rural areas. The northwest submission in particular refers to the need for developing a number of major urban poles as a counterbalance to the pull of Dublin. However, this remains a vague aspiration without mention of any specific towns – which probably points to the political difficulties involved in operationalising the proposal. A more specific proposal on development poles in relation to manufacturing industry and services is contained in the submission by the Irish Congress of Trade Unions (ICTU).

Instead of advocating a form of growth centre policy, which is what is implied in the northwest submission, and that of ICTU, the submissions from the southwest and midlands/east recommend an area-based approach. Their concern is to find a way that enables them to prioritise objectives in order to choose measures, and, second, to group together the measures in coherent packages. The response suggested to these two issues is an area-based approach which is designed to see how national priorities can assist in the development of the sub-region and how the sub-region can assist national development. In their programmes, the primary means of grouping measures is on a spatial basis. The sectoral components of the programmes are made 'subservient' to the concept of area development. The premise underlying this approach is that every area of the sub-region has potential which remains to be exploited. It also recognises that every area does not have the same amount of potential and that measures should be implemented that are appropriate to the extent and nature of the potential that does exist.

The National Development Plan 1994–9

The second National Development Plan to cover the period until the end of the decade was published towards the end of 1993 and simultaneously submitted to Brussels for consideration. Negotiations between officials in Dublin and Brussels have been on-going so that the final form of the next Community Support Framework remains to be decided (1994).

This section briefly summarises some key aspects of the plan relevant to regional development in Ireland. The plan has two central objectives: first, to ensure the best long-term return for the economy by increasing output, economic potential and long-term jobs and, second, to reintegrate the long-term unemployed, and those at high risk of becoming so, into the economic mainstream. Its strategy is essentially top-down, based on a number of sectoral programmes, which have some significance for regional development. For example, the chapter on industry devotes a lengthy section to its role in regional development, while the chapter on infrastructure proposes several measures that are intended to address the current imbalance in sub-regional networks. In addition to the sectoral proposals there is provision for a special programme on local development. The final chapter is titled 'Sub-regional Aspects'. It summarises the main concerns raised by the sub-regional review groups and indicates how they are addressed by the programmes outlined in the plan. The approach adopted here is a considerable improvement on that of the first plan. Another welcome feature of the second plan is a commitment that its implementation 'will be undertaken in a manner which fully respects the principle of environment sustainability' (1994, p. 31). Finally, the plan acknowledges the need for new institutional arrangements including County Enterprise Boards and statutorily established Regional Authorities.

While there are many positive features in the new plan, including a commitment to a more broadly defined concept of development, there are a number of issues that require further attention. The proposed local development programme is too narrowly focused on enterprise creation without sufficient attention to developing appropriate software (Martinos, 1989). A detailed critique of the proposals in this area has already been published by the National Economic and Social Forum (1993). The proposals on transport are designed to improve interaction between regions in Ireland. However, improved inter-regional transport networks can only make a limited contribution to regional development. Consideration must also be given to the settlement pattern and whether specific interventions are required to alter it.

Conclusion

The 1988 reform of the EC Structural Funds provided an opportunity for a major refocusing of strategies aimed at alleviating the extent of regional disparities in the Community. For the member states there was a challenge provided to devise a multi-annual plan consisting of integrated programmes. Partnership was intended to be a key component in the preparation, financing, monitoring and assessment of the support framework.

The experience under the first CSF was mixed. On the one hand, a new planning process involving greater consultation was initiated which would probably not have occurred without prompting from Brussels. The requirement that a National Development Plan be prepared in order to seek Structural Funds, the introduction of the partnership principle (notwithstanding the very limited way in which it has been applied), the sub-regional component, the requirement that reviews be carried out and the process of inviting submissions have all been very positive outcomes. The preparation of submissions by many different interest groups has probably been an important learning experience for each group, given that they have been obliged to analyse the development process from their own perspective and identify their priorities. The key points of many of the submissions have been covered in the media which provides an indication of the divergent range of priorities that the central administrators have eventually to attempt to reconcile. In a sense a shared learning process has been started.

The availability of a substantial amount of funds from the EU along with the inputs from the national government and the private sector have resulted in a considerable amount of investment which has brought many benefits in relation to the quality of physical infrastructure, improving the natural environment and provision of employment. The allocation of expenditure between the sub-regions in Ireland has also been biased in favour of the areas of greatest need.

On the other hand, there have been a number of problems. The basic principle of partnership has not been effectively developed. The sub-regional review committees are severely restrained in their actions. In practice, most of the Structural Funds are channelled through the Department of Finance. They are spent on sectoral programmes through the mainline departments in exactly the same way that assistance under the separate funds prior to 1988 was allocated. Essentially, the government has continued to use the mechanisms that were already in place, with existing agencies being called upon to implement programmes that in many cases were already in place. Essentially there has been very little change to the way in which interventions in the development process are organised. There has also been insufficient coordination of activities at different geographical scales. This has resulted in negative outcomes such as restricted exploitation of land resources, environmental damage and at times wasteful use of resources. It has also contributed to a number of unhelpful controversies as, for example, between conservationists and developers and between some rural and urban interests.

In order to maximise the benefits to Ireland from the next round of EU Structural Funds, it is essential that careful attention be given to the development process. It must be seen as not only an economic process but as one which also involves social, political and environmental objectives. More attention should be directed to reducing the extent of disparities between regions and social groups in Ireland than to the larger objective of achieving convergence with the more affluent regions in other parts of the EU. The persistence of regional and social inequalities, after decades of intervention measures by Irish governments and the EU, suggests that it is time to seek a new paradigm for regional analysis. The concept of development must be broadened. The present institutional framework is dominated by top-down agencies which are related to a highly centralised administrative system that has not been able to achieve coordination of policies across departments. While the National Development Plan for 1994–9 attempts to address some of the fundamental problems much remains to be done. Sustainable local and regional development will require new structures that will facilitate empowerment and participation through partnership, adopt a multidimensional and flexible approach, and permit both horizontal and vertical integration of policy measures. The local and regional dimension must not be seen as just an adjunct to the overall process of planning for development; rather it must be seen as a central component which incorporates the processes that influence social and spatial outcomes.

Notes

1. The measures to be assisted under the CSF are grouped in relation to four specific priorities:

   (i) Agriculture, fisheries, forestry, tourism and rural development
   (ii) Industry and services
   (iii) Measures to offset the effects of peripherality
   (iv) Human resources measures.

2. The areas of priority are as follows: agriculture, fisheries, tourism and rural development; industry and services; measures to offset the effects of peripherality and human resources.

5

Economic Development: A Trade Union Response

PAUL SWEENEY

A major obstacle to the development of the Republic's economy is that economists and policy makers have continuously focused on the wrong problems. For example, at company level they are obsessed with labour costs, with a consequent serious neglect of the real determinants of competitiveness. Moreover, new ways of working in the factory or office have also been largely ignored. At national level, policy makers have overemphasised the role of foreign investment on the one hand and neglected the impact of transfer price-fixing by transnationals on the other. The nature of these conceptual fallacies are further highlighted by the dichotomy between the ruling ideology of free market economics and the practice of very high levels of state intervention and subsidisation of private capital. In sum this intervention has not been successful, except in holding employment steady, while unemployment rises.

There are a whole range of opportunities and alternative policy making structures which should be applied in order adequately to challenge the socio-economic crisis now evident in the Republic. However, as argued in this chapter, an effective socio-economic development profile must be tied not only to job creation but also to a consensus at national level that technology and enterprise should be combined in order to expand new ways of working.

New Ways of Working

Most Irish trade unionists now recognise that some of the new developments on the factory floor, which increase productivity and the competitiveness of firms, can also have a liberating effect upon workers, empowering them and involving them in decision-making, if implemented in a correct and democratic manner. While Human Resource Management (HRM) is cynically used by some managements simply to boost productivity, the need for greater quality and for on-going innovation has led to the more progressive managements realising that Taylorist production methods are no longer appropriate if a company is to be competitive. A central issue in reversing the labour shedding and deskilling tendencies of Taylorist methods is the continual inclusion of employees as active participants within the production process. Active participation by trade unions in these changes can lead to improved conditions, pay and job security for trade union members.

The move from mass production toward the post-Fordist emphasis on mass customisation means that there must be relentless attention to quality, team-working and J-I-T delivery. The flattening of the pyramidal structure of the firm means that there is less supervision and workers can determine their own pace, hours and intensity of work. These are currents which trade unions are better working with than against. Moreover, it should also be accepted by employers that technology is not neutral and it must be used to reduce working time in order to free workers from boring tasks, with the rewards of altering work-cycles being fairly distributed (Gorz, 1989).

In many ways TNCs have re-evaluated their previous employment policies. Increased global competition, with a premium on price, quality and responsiveness to customer needs, has promoted rapidly changing technologies which emphasise the need for flexible and adaptable organisations and workforces. A distinct supply-side crisis is presently underway and is reflected in the decline of working-class positions. An analysis by ICTU (1993) identified a number of competitive pressures which led to the introduction of workplace reorganisation. There has been a general trend to increase productivity and reduce unit costs through introducing more flexible responses. It is argued that traditional Taylorist and Fordist approaches to work organisation were incapable of producing significant productivity gains and reduced unit costs.

Some firms have recognised that it is vitally important to harness the collective intelligence of their workforce through greater participation at all levels of decision-making, if they are to remain competitive and innovative. There is an important role for trade unions in ensuring that the new ways of working, which lead to greater competitiveness of firms, also emancipate workers from drudgery, reduce working time and ensure that the profits are shared. This is why Irish trade unions are participating on the factory floor in these developments (ICTU, 1993). The marketplace and technological change are forcing the pace of change which must be channelled in progressive ways.

In Ireland, the overall level of competitiveness can be increased by adopting new ways of working. Autonomous work groups, flexible specialisation, process re-engineering and all the other advanced production and management techniques should be examined as potential contributions to employment growth. However, it is important that productive reorganisation is based upon consensus between management, workers and the state.

Competitiveness, Pay and Unemployment

Competitiveness is of vital importance not just to employers but also to employees. For the political right, competitiveness is often incorrectly reduced to an overemphasis upon labour costs. Competitiveness is a complex matter and is determined by other important factors such as product quality, reliability and price of products. Analysis of competitiveness should also take account of a country's market dynamism, the quality of human resources, development of infrastructure, natural resources, product innovation, political stability, the strength of the banking and investment sectors, and the role of the state in encouraging enterprise (Best, 1990).

In 1981, the Irish government commissioned a group of three economists (known as the 'Three Wise Men') to look at the area of competitiveness in the Republic's economy (Committee on Costs and Competitiveness, 1981). The overall thrust of the Committee's findings (and the basis of their most recent individual work) was that pay increases should be set substantially lower than inflation in order to ensure that income policies would move wages closer to the market clearing wage during periods of high unemployment (McAleese, 1993; Walsh, 1993). In other words, wages must be reduced substantially and then unemployment will be cleared away. In general, these economic fundamentals have been very good, and often excellent, but unemployment has grown rapidly and inexorably, demonstrating that the policy-making orthodoxy is seriously flawed.

Traditionally, and particularly in the early 1980s, when inflation was high, workers were told that if real wage reductions were tied to productivity gains then employment would ultimately increase. However, in reality, significant national productivity growth rates have not been accompanied by a rise in the rate of employment growth. For example, every 1 per cent growth in GNP in Ireland between 1950 and 1990 was associated with a pathetic average growth of 0.08 per cent in employment. This ratio was the lowest of all European OECD countries during the same period (NESC, 1992; Shirlow, 1994). The failure of extensive productivity growth to create significant employment gains must in turn be set against the fact that Irish wage costs are not particularly high by international standards and are amongst the lowest within the EU. Furthermore, significant decreases in real unit labour costs have actually been accompanied by a three-fold increase in the level of unemployment. As shown in Table 5.1, Irish real unit labour costs have fallen by 14.2 per cent since 1980. This significant decrease in real unit labour costs is nearly double the average decrease of 7.8 per cent for all EU countries.

Table 5.1 Real Unit Labour Costs 1993 (Base: 1980 = 100)

Nation	*Luxembourg*	*UK*	*Italy*	*Germany*	*Belgium*	*France*
Unit Cost	99.6	98.4	95.2	92.1	92.0	89.5
Nation	*Netherlands*	*Greece*	*Denmark*	*Ireland*	*Portugal*	*Spain*
Unit Cost	88.6	88.5	88.4	85.8	84.4	84.4

Source: *European Economy* (1993).

As demonstrated by the evidence contained in Table 5.1, the Republic's economy has outcompeted the majority of its competitors in relation to wage control and productivity growth, but unfortunately has not produced significant social benefits. The negative relationship between real unit labour cost reduction and unemployment growth further highlights the inadequacy of orthodox economic analysis. Lower wages and higher productivity levels clearly do not mean more jobs in a modern, peripheral and open economy such as Ireland. What they do mean are higher profit rates, particularly among the technologically sophisticated, modern manufacturing sectors.

Free Market Ideology and Reality

Irish economists focus largely on micro issues and while interest rates, inflation rates and balance of payment terms are important issues, governments of peripheral economies have only a small and declining influence over them. A coherent strategy to improve firms' competitiveness in the ways dealt with here is the key to increasing employment, assuming that macro issues are competently managed. However, before such issues can be adequately addressed it is vital to challenge the contradiction between free market ideology and the actuality of a heavily interventionist economic system. The level of state intervention in Ireland is very high in comparison to other EU and main competitor states. In addition to tax breaks, there are many state agencies which are almost totally devoted to assisting the private sector. State intervention has not been disastrous in the Republic, but it has been very expensive and relatively ineffective. In Ireland, there has been an extraordinarily high level of state intervention in industry, in the hope of jobs, with little serious monitoring of the efficiency of such intervention. This is part of the dichotomy between *laissez-faire* economic theory and interventionist practice. There has been a 'business-man's dole mentality' in Ireland, where supposed entrepreneurs are more successful in getting grants and subsidies from the state than they are in generating profits (Keating and Desmond, 1993). For example, the *Culliton Report* highlighted the fact that a total of £1.6 billion in grants alone went to the industrial sector with the creation of a mere 7000 net new jobs in the 1980s (Industrial Policy Review Group, 1992). Moreover, during the same period the gross cost of tax expenditures amounted to £7 billion (Sweeney, 1992). The net cost of the tax breaks is considerably less than this, but it is still very high.

Understanding the nature of this dichotomy is vitally important. If we do not have a very clear understanding of the way in which the state intervenes in the economy, then that intervention will not be effective. The fallacy of free marketeering combined within ineffective state planning must be replaced by a policy of confronting socio-economic issues in a planned way, rather than waiting for the right 'climate' and other divine interventions. Markets are created by people, regulated by people and can be made to serve people. Our own interventions require change. For example, policy makers and economists in the Republic have traditionally hidden behind the rapid growth in the labour force as an excuse for their failure on the employment front. Yet an examination of labour-force growth shows that it has not been a problem, especially in the last decade, because of mass emigration. While the average non-agricultural employment growth of 1.3 per cent per annum in the thirty years to 1990 is considerably better than the EC performance of 0.9 per cent, it is still below the OECD average of 1.6 per cent per annum. Yet because of mass emigration in the 1980s, the Republic's labour-force growth, at only 0.2 per cent a year, was well below other industrial countries. Moreover, during the 1980s, Ireland's labour-force growth rate was two thirds lower than the EU average. As such, the unemployment crisis cannot simply be blamed on labour-force growth.

The high birth rate in the Republic is, of course, a product of the policy of successive conservative governments, which up to very recently slavishly followed the directions of the Catholic Church. Initially, rapid labour-force growth looks like a powerful argument for inertia because of the extent of the problem, with over 30,000 additional jobs required each year, if employment is to be reduced to 100,000 by 2000. This was the objective of the 1990 Programme of 'Economic and Social Progress'. Alternatively, 20,000 new jobs are required to hold unemployment at its current, unacceptably high level. In practice, only 4000 new jobs have been created on average each year over the past three years.[1]

No matter how high the demographic demands are, a government's employment policy should be geared up to meeting them. Official reports have shown that one third of the Republic's people live in poverty (Callen et al., 1987). Other studies have shown that the most effective way of dealing with poverty is to provide employment opportunities (Callen et al., 1989). This only underlines the necessity for employment policies which are both sustainable and equitable.

Manufacturing is Still the Key!

It is widely recognised that most jobs will be in the service sector, but these will be dependent on the wealth generated in the manufacturing sector. Thus, the manufacturing sector is still the key to employment. Even after adjustment for transfer pricing, the share of manufacturing in the Republic's economic growth between 1986 and 1990 was higher than in thirteen other countries, including Japan (NESC, 1992). In 1982, the *Telesis Report*, commissioned by the NESC, set out the agenda for Irish industrial policy (Telesis Consultancy Group, 1982). The key recommendation was to focus on indigenous industry with a reduction in grants to foreign firms. While this report was strongly opposed by the Industrial Development Authority and many key decision-makers, eventually many of its recommendations were actually implemented. This has benefited Irish industry.

In January 1992, ten years later, the *Culliton Report* was welcomed by virtually everybody concerned with industrial policy. Culliton which should be addressed by policy makers. Profit and royalty outflows amount to £IR3300 million or 14.6 per cent of GDP in 1994, a massive haemorrhage from the manufacturing sector and a major factor in low employment growth within the economy. Too little attention has been paid to this by policy makers who, embarrassed by it, simply ignore it.

Manufacturing: The Global Context

There have been many positive developments for the Republic as a member of the EU, but there are a number of issues which are neglected. First, when the current transfer of Structural Funds runs out, it is unlikely that Ireland will enjoy anywhere near as many transfers because of the competing claims of Eastern and other peripheral European countries. Second, the EU budget at 1.2 per cent of Community GDP in 1993 is very small for a federal union of states. There is a strong case for a greatly expanded EU budget. Third, a high proportion of the funds still goes to the Common Agricultural Policy, where 80 per cent of funds have been going to the top 20 per cent of farmers. Fourth, the 'democratic deficit', or lack of democracy, means that power resides with the Commission which is known to be out of touch with the people of Europe (after the Irish, Danish and French referenda).

The EU Structural Funds, which help in modernising the Republic's infrastructure, represent substantial intervention in the economy. But, they are far from sufficient to achieve convergence. Irish GDP per worker has risen considerably since Ireland joined the EU, from 69 per cent of the union average in 1973 to 89 per cent in 1990. However, because of Ireland's high dependency ratio, the rise in GNP per capita has only been from 59 per cent to 62 per cent (Kennedy, 1992; 1993b). This is largely as a result of high unemployment. In order to reverse unemployment growth trends there should be concerted action by the 'twelve' on unemployment in Europe (where the average rate of unemployment will top 11 per cent or 20 million by the end of 1994) through a planned Keynesian-style intervention. Such intervention was suggested in the early drafts of Delors' White Paper on unemployment in late 1993, but the member states refused to fully implement its policy recommendations. Furthermore, Irish industrial policy must be part of an integrated and coherent EU-wide interventionist industrial policy. This could play a far more important role in convergence than the Structural and Cohesion Funds. Instead of

refined Telesis and broadened its scope to embrace
education policy and other areas. However, it failed
industrial policy in the European context and while q
subsidies to industry, totally neglected to quantify the
breaks. A negative feature of the debate on Culliton has
attention has been focused on the state agencies ar
industrial enterprises. The Fianna Fail Labour gove
response to the *Culliton Report*, published in a formal rep
Employment Through Enterprise (Department of Enter
Employment, 1993) indicated that the *Culliton Report*
effectively buried. This is extremely regrettable. If we
back to Culliton/Telesis then we would have the basic pr
to develop indigenous industry, which is the key t
generation. Wealth which may be retained in the cour

Foreign Investment

Irish trade unions support foreign investment. But we h
accepted the Telesis thesis that we should focus on in
enterprise and that we have over-relied on foreign investm
Transport and General Workers Union, 1981–8). A further
has been the creation of a dual economy in Ireland
high-tech, high export, high productivity industries do
by foreign companies, while Irish-owned companies have
ductivity rates, low wage rates, and a low share of exp
example, 68.5 per cent of Irish-controlled employment i
upon the low-value added sectors compared to 35.5
among foreign companies (Shirlow, 1994).[2] Duality is co
with an overdependence upon foreign investment largely
of the lack of development (actually the shrinkage) of inc
industry and increased levels of profit repatriation. It wa
earlier that Irish workers' productivity growth has been v
and, indeed, it has substantially surpassed most indus
countries, including Japan, by output per employee in th
(NESC, 1992). However, there is a problem with som
official statistics, and particularly that key statistic, the
growth, and more specifically, the rate of growth of Gross D
Product (GDP).

Ireland's GDP has been exaggerated because of transf
fixing by transnational companies which locate profit here
to enjoy the low corporate tax regimes. As GDP is the c
for debt/GDP ratios and the Maastricht criteria, this is a p

a begging bowl, we should seek Union assistance to help us to create sustainable jobs. While, in theory, state intervention may not be popular in Europe, it is just as significant in practice as it is in Ireland. The level of industrial subsidies in Germany is 22 times that of the Republic (EC, 1992).

Furthermore, it is essential that the EU deals with TNCs as a Community or Union which seeks to develop its peripheral areas as part of a coherent industrial policy by, for example, arbitrating on an inter-regional basis. A coherent strategy regarding TNCs would reduce the possibility of peripheral areas continually competing for overseas investment. Another European concern is the Single European Market's emphasis on 'free competition'. Too often this means the dominance of the largest firms, which are the most 'competitive' because of economies of scale and scope. In order to counter-balance such market excesses, it is vital that the Social Chapter is implemented with vigour.

If the political right dominate the EU, part of the reason is that on the left the social democratic governments in Europe have no valid structures capable of tackling unemployment due to a continual avoidance of radical policies on job creation. The intellectual hegemony of the right, brought about by the Thatcher/Reagan era, the collapse of the Soviet Union and the globalisation of the world economy, through massive deregulation (which appeared to be 'inevitable'), have deflated the left. While the basic ideas of socialists are more relevant than ever, the proponents of these ideas, particularly where they have power, appear to have a severe problem of confidence.

Conclusion

The fundamental key in the Irish economy is job creation. Governments have singularly failed in this area since the foundation of the Republic in 1922. There are 10 per cent less at work now in the Republic than at independence. Never has there been a better opportunity than at present to grapple with the staggering level of unemployment of 21 per cent, or 300,000, unemployed. We have just negotiated the third programme, the Programme for Competitiveness and Work (PCW) and there is a government with the largest majority ever. With such a substantial consensus, the objective should be to mobilise the whole economy in a war against unemployment. However, the cynic might say that with such a strong neo-corporatist alliance, the 'culture of contentment' may predominate. All institutions, particularly the state itself, tend towards conservatism and the status quo: they oppose change, particularly radical change. The level of unemployment in Ireland is so high that it requires radical solutions and action by virtually all institutions in the state, from the state itself, its many institutions, trade unions, professional organisations, and all interest groups, down to individuals.

The main losers with mass unemployment are the unemployed, most of whom have the lowest educational qualifications, one third of whom are thoroughly demoralised, having been unemployed for more than a year, all of whom are in relative poverty, none of whom have any discretionary income and a great proportion of whom do not even vote. This means that the key political institution in the state is the government. It can effect the change through committed leadership of all its institutions and other institutions, including unions, companies and individuals. However, as this is the era of the professional rather than the committed politician, the likelihood of a real concerted war on unemployment in the Republic is negligible. Such criticism is not based on ideological point scoring but instead is centred on stimulating a debate which is capable of mobilising the whole economy on a war footing against unemployment. It is evident in recent years that the majority of trade unionists, if convinced that the programme for such a war was serious and was developed by consensus, would be willing to play their part and to accept changes. If a war on unemployment is to be successful, it will be painful for all in the short term. All, except those on low incomes, should share these changes proportionately.

I have dealt with some economic problems which, I believe, have been neglected by economists and policy makers in Ireland when dealing with unemployment. It has been argued that conventional economists concentrate too much on macro issues over which we have decreasing influence in a small economy. This criticism is centred on (what I believe to be) a robust trade union perspective, but one which is not dogmatic and, in the spirit of consensus, is open to criticism, amendment and change. At the level of the firm, criticism must be directed at the overemphasis by economists on the supply side, specifically labour costs and related areas. Labour costs can be important, particularly in services, but we must also look at the overall complexity of competitiveness.

Radical changes are transforming many workplaces, where workers are being liberated from repetitive and boring work, being given autonomy and participating in innovation, in enhancing quality and in decision-making. These developments are opportunities for firms to make quantum leaps in competitiveness and ultimately in job creation. Our excellently educated workforce, rapidly declining communication and transport costs, the small size of our industrial base, and the acceptance by trade unionists and others of the need for change, are the basis on which to build indigenous and innovative manufacturing, which is still the key to solving unemployment. But we must take a long-term perspective and deal with areas of disagreement. At the level of the state there has to be an acceptance that Ireland is not a *laissez-faire* or free market economy and that policy is heavily interventionist. EU policy, in Structural and Cohesion Funds and CAP is also interventionist. Therefore, the focus must be on the quality of intervention and on value for money. If necessary, we will have to cut the 'business-man's dole'!

The increased globalisation of competition, the anarchy in capital markets in 1992–3 and the collapse of the Soviet Union have led many to believe that the nation state cannot intervene successfully in the economy. While many trends, both technological and political (such as deregulation and removal of exchange controls) have lessened the impact of sovereign governments, the level of intervention by government is at its highest ever. The EU must be developed as a real Community or Union of its member states, with larger budgets, a Union industrial policy, a vigorous social policy (which retains the best of the social and economic progress achieved by Europe this century), and there must be EU demand-management, when required. It is the role of the government to provide the necessary leadership. Its response to the *Culliton Report* and its failure to meet even the extremely modest job targets of the 'Programme for Economic and Social Progress' do not auger well for such a war effort. The government appears to be contented. Is it awaiting the upturn in the international economy and the resumption of emigration?

Notes

1. The dramatic fall in the Republic's birth rate since 1980 means that employment requirements will fall from 30,000 new jobs a year to only 6000 in 2005. In 1993, the total female fertility rate in the Republic had fallen dramatically to 1.97, the lowest in Europe and below replacement level. This means

that a labour-force shortage may be the problem early in the next century.

2. The definition of low and high value added sectors is based on IDA and SFADCo employment surveys 1993. It excludes data from the Udaras na Gaeltachta area. Low value added sectors include: drink and tobacco, timber and furniture, textiles, non-metallic materials, clothing and footwear, miscellaneous, printing and paper sectors. High value added sectors include: rubber and plastics, chemicals, electrical and mechanical engineering, instrument engineering, metals, office machinery products.

6

Industrial Collapse and Post-Fordist Overdetermination of Belfast

ANDREAS CEBULLA AND JIM SMITH

In Belfast there are two interlinked processes which determine the nature of urban policy. First, the weakness of private institutions and the absence of effective regulation of the economy have set parameters on the type of economic development chosen by policy makers. Second, urban policy has been heavily influenced by the dictates of conflict management and military strategy in the face of protracted internal war. Both of these factors, and urban policy in general, have been subordinated to larger global processes of industrial decline, restructuring and capital migration which have had an impact upon every region and city of the developed world. This chapter describes the significance of the management of space to economic development policies in a sectarian society and highlights the underlying obstacles to successful reform of outmoded structures. It will be argued that inevitably these factors co-determined the type of regeneration pursued in the city of Belfast which led to a 'boosterist' presentation of regeneration efforts as opposed to a coordinated, thoughtful approach to social and economic improvement. In effect, the state, through its policies, has manipulated the urban class structure, without addressing the fundamental issues which divide the city and truncate its economic development, i.e. social inequity and exclusion combined with ethnic division.

Economic Decline and Government Response

Until the late 1960s Belfast was the centre of industrial production in Northern Ireland. The city's industrial basis emerged in the nineteenth century around shipbuilding and textiles. Both these industries – and the ancillary engineering sector – were resistant to Fordist production methods and went into rapid decline after

1960 under competition from low wage economies and as a result of the failure of local capital to embark on restructuring and recapitalisation. The linen industry is a case in point. Between 1958 and 1964 one third of the linen plants in Northern Ireland closed down with a loss of 27,000 jobs or 45 per cent of the workforce. According to a report commissioned by the government of Northern Ireland in 1955, the indirect evidence suggested that levels of investment (in Northern Ireland) in production and trade were 'substantially less, per head of population than in Britain' (Isles and Cuthbert, 1957, p. 155) and they further concluded that '... there is a remarkably strong tendency for people in Northern Ireland to invest their capital outside the province' (ibid., p. 158).

Recent debate on the development of the post-colonial state has highlighted the important role of the emerging native bourgeoisie in achieving indigenous growth (Amin, 1992; Mansour, 1992). It would appear that, in Northern Ireland, the circumstances of the birth of this state prevented the emergence and growth of an indigenous bourgeoisie with local rather than British ties and outlook. The Protestant middle classes showed little interest in building and sustaining an independent nation or region within a nation. Instead, their main concern was to consolidate power structures at the local, i.e. town or parish, level. There, power was built not just on absolute economic wealth, but on a dominant structure of selective favouritism which had been inherited from previous generations. Privilege (within the Union, as well as within the region) reinforced and sustained sectarian identity and formed the basis for the consolidation of the Northern Irish state.

Democratic state structures and civil society based on consensus and legitimacy could not emerge in a society which was forced to rely on the coercion and marginalisation of the minority population combined with privilege bargaining between Protestant capital and the Protestant working class. The decline of manufacturing industry, which accelerated after the Second World War, challenged the dominance of Protestant labour. As the regional economic structure began to crumble, crucial elements within Unionism resisted demands for reform, fearing the political consequences. The reforming wing of Unionism, however, believed that the introduction of Fordist-type industry and technocratic planning could stabilise an increasingly volatile situation. Attempts on the part of government agencies to revitalise industry by attracting outside capital had some initial success but soon foundered on the rock of world recession and international competition. In the past, the sectarian nature of the state reduced the pressure on local industry to adopt modern (post-Fordist) production techniques. In more recent years, government policy reverted to generous financial support measures to stimulate economic activity. In part, this was a concession to the private sector, whose poor performance government interpreted, or at least presented, as resulting from politically motivated violence. Intimidated by the city's violent image, and concerned to present a counter image of industrial success, state development agencies pulled back from attaching and enforcing conditions to the recipients of its support packages. The 'sectarian cushion' and government subsidisation of the economy had a similar effect, in that it relieved industry from the need to 'benchmark' its activities in order to generate wealth. Teague (1993a) has shown that the British subvention has had a malign impact on the economy. He points to recent evidence of state grant assistance to manufacturing in Northern Ireland being used to ensure business profitability without improvements in productivity and market positions (cp. NIERC, 1993a, 1993b).

Successive governments failed effectively to address the underlying problem of social relations in the region. Government reluctance to regulate, as opposed to subsidising of, society and economy inhibited the reform of social relations which had been critical in promoting labour market segmentation and social inequality. To date, access to education and employment (and employment promotion) remains mediated by religious institutions or by simple fact of religious affiliation. The state has relieved the private sector from acknowledging its role in Northern Ireland's economic decline. Instead, the 'troubles' have been blamed for the region's continued economic problems.

Urban Policy and Conflict Management

Traces of an attempt to regulate the urban economy can be found in the early 1960s. In 1964, the Belfast Regional Survey and Plan (named the *Matthew Plan* after its author) was published. The plan was technocratic in its approach with the overall objective of making recommendations about the reorganisation of space in Belfast to facilitate Fordist-type economic growth. Matthew concluded that there was a general lack of provision for the growing and evolving needs of a modern industrial economy and the 'dilapidation' of central Belfast, combined with an intolerable situation of 'unregulated sprawl' forbade the siting of new industry in the city. His solution was in line with international thinking at the time: industry was to be located in new 'growth centres' and large areas of the traditional city were to be demolished to make way for a road and motorway network.

The plan (and the *Transportation Plan* which followed in its wake) was 'apolitically political' (Blair, 1973, p. 162) in that it was an attempt to introduce rational planning and technocratic coercion without consideration of the reality of a city deeply divided on ethnic lines. The *Matthew Plan* was never fully implemented. Instead there was a piecemeal and pragmatic approach to the twin pressures of economic downturn and growing civil unrest. The former undermined the optimistic predictions of economic and population growth, whereas local opposition to the massive destruction of working-class communities encouraged by the *Matthew Plan* attained a political dimension in the context of large-scale civil unrest and inter-communal conflict. The two communities were united and largely successful in their opposition to the more grandiose road plans (Wiener, 1980).

The latest spell of civil unrest in Northern Ireland has had its origins in an initially peaceful protest against continued discrimination by the local state against the Catholic minority. In the early days of the conflict, its geographical centre in Belfast was along community intersections in the west and inner east of the city. Essentially there are two types of space in Belfast: sectarian space which is defined by the domination and control of one community, and neutral space where members of both communities can mix in accordance with agreed rules.[1] The civil unrest which began in 1969 led to a disruption of this division of space, in the first instance through the Civil Rights marches and later as a result of the bombing campaign of the IRA against commercial targets. This bombing campaign challenged the fake neutrality of city centre space.

In 1972, the British government imposed Direct Rule over the region from Westminster. During the 1970s it attempted to reconcile two strands of policy: an increasingly sophisticated counter-insurgency strategy designed to eliminate the threat from the IRA and other groups, and an urban policy aimed at alleviating the deprivation which was seen as a breeding ground for political violence. The publication of the *Belfast Areas of Social Need* report, (1976), identified large parts of Belfast which suffered from multiple deprivation. The response of the state was to increase spending to alleviate social and economic problems. Attempts were made to attract industry to locate in deprived areas and there was a mushrooming of leisure and community centres, youth clubs, etc. across the city.

This carrot of state intervention was balanced by the stick of military occupation and the emergence of an increasingly repressive and sophisticated legal and security apparatus. The city centre became a fortress, surrounded by a ring of steel to keep out the bombers. The British state seemed to believe during this period that, given the right combination of measures, a return to economic growth and a regeneration of traditional industry was possible. The assumption also was that the reversal of economic decline would equally eliminate the threat of communal violence lingering in Belfast. The considerable investment in infrastructure and social/leisure projects brought about little change in the distribution of social deprivation and did nothing to draw support away from the IRA in nationalist areas. This was the implication of the 1981 update of the 1976 *Belfast Areas of Social Need* report (PPRU, 1988).

The level of support for the IRA hunger strikes of 1980–1 gave the lie to the official line that support for militant nationalism was minimal. The subsequent successes of Sinn Fein in elections seems to have temporarily convinced the state that there was nothing to gain by attempting to win over a significant section of the nationalist population. The Anglo-Irish Agreement of 1985 was the political expression of this view in that it attempted to isolate Sinn Fein and strengthen the hand of constitutional nationalism. Economic policy shifted away from large capital projects towards targeting specific groups and the coopting of local organisations (such as the Catholic Church) to act as conduits for funding and to police its distribution.[2]

Urban Regeneration Policy in the 1980s

Public money flowed back into areas of need after the killing of two British soldiers in west Belfast in 1987 had alerted the state (and the private sector) to the need again to address the grievances endured by the west and north Belfast population. Policy initiatives were devised to improve access to government funds and government departments were given extra funds for expenditure projects in disadvantaged areas. Whereas a special policy initiative was launched in the north and west of the city, this was a mere cosmetic exercise compared to the effort expended, in both financial and political terms, to create an area of conspicuous consumption in the city core. The thoroughness with which the task of inner city regeneration was pursued is attested to by the fact that between 1984 and 1991, all employment growth in the city took place within a one mile radius of the central business district. Employment in all other parts of the city fell by about the same amount. This type of urban regeneration, of course, was very much in line with more international trends. But in Belfast, the creation of an image of normality and consumerist activity in the face of an on-going armed conflict was as important as presenting city centre investment as a new approach to the alleviation of economic and social problems.

The regeneration strategy came about as a result of the adoption of policies already in operation in Great Britain, further fuelled by strong lobbying on the part of local traders in Belfast's city centre. During the 1970s, planners and industrial developers were forced to accept virtually any type of development proposal that was offered in order to attract or consolidate any potential source of employment at all. Generous aid to manufacturing industry removed the need for industry to organise effectively in order to look after their own needs. In any case, they were reluctant to invest in the first place and thus unlikely candidates for constituting a lobby. But most importantly, government made no concerted effort to include manufacturing in its attempts to turn around the city economy. This task was made even more difficult by the internationalisation of the urban economy. During the 1980s, major manufacturing business in Belfast had been taken over by the externally owned corporations.[3] While rescuing many of them from impending closure, internationalisation also detached the business sector from the locality. Retailers and property developers, on the other hand, retained their interest in the well-being of the local economy. The urban retail sector had a particularly strong interest in the regeneration of Belfast as the emergence of a ring of suburban shopping developments in the 1970s threatened the viability of city centre trade.

The bombing campaign against commercial property during the first half of the 1970s had led to the destruction of almost one quarter of the total city centre floorspace (Brown, 1985). Measures to protect the rest led to a further downturn in economic activity. There is an irony in the consequences of the IRA bombing campaign which had the stated objective of undermining capitalism and imperialism in the North. In effect, the bombing campaign helped lay the foundations for the profitable rebuilding of Belfast as – when the bombing receded towards the end of the 1970s and early 1980s – traders called for help in city centre reinvestment and planners discovered the purchasing power of the suburban middle classes, which had been largely unaffected by the 'troubles'.

This shift in urban policy was to gain a highly political significance. Redeveloping the city centre (in Belfast and other cities in the North) was presented by the state as a sign of 'caring' for the population and a symbol of resistance against the destructive power of the bomber. City centre redevelopment was presented as a means of providing employment opportunities in an area which 'offers easy accessibility to all sections of the urban populations' (*Belfast Urban Area Plan*, 1987, p. 13). For 'all sections of the urban population' read, in particular sections from the disadvantaged, high unemployment areas of north and west Belfast.

The need to attract investors to fund both the reconstruction and to fill the retail and office space created affected the public presentation of life in Belfast. Above all, the official interpretation of the causes of poor economic development had to change in tune with the turnaround in urban policy. Previously, the blame for economic stagnation and decline was laid squarely at the door of the 'terrorists' who were held responsible for the lack of inward investment and the destruction of jobs. The failure of such measures such as the ring-fencing of the city centre was attributed, by the state, to the level of political violence in that economic regeneration was impossible as long as civil disorder existed. This, however, amounted to a tacit admission that the policy of 'normalisation' pursued since the mid-1970s had failed and it created an image of a strife-torn province which acted as a disincentive to investors. Nor did the strategy solve the problem of defeating the IRA; they merely switched targets.

Constructing a Post-Industrial Urban Class Structure

The imposition of Direct Rule on Northern Ireland had a profound impact on the shape of ethnic and class relations in Belfast. Direct Rule coincided with local government reforms in the UK which, together with the establishment of a new strata of 'nationally' governed administrators in the region, brought with it a wave of public sector recruitment. Whereas, as Teague (1993a) has demonstrated, the state has not been able to exert any real influence on, and impose a mode of regulation of, private investors, it has established a new (cross community) service class which pledges allegiance to the British state as well as the status quo. State intervention and the high level of subsidy had the desired political effect of consolidating a buffer class tied by self-interest to the British state. The state did not create this class, but its 'normalisation' policy[4] gave it a numerical and political significance which it would not have attained had the level of central state expenditure not been so high.

Urban regeneration has been a public sector-led undertaking. The failure to incorporate the private sector, and to formally redress the equity balance in the city, for fear of raising the regional constitutional question, put the state into its current position as a regulator of social, rather than economic, relations. The chief effect of industrial policy was to create a 'workhouse economy' (Rowthorn, 1987, p. 117) in Northern Ireland where the majority of the population are in receipt of a state subsidy in some form or another. The state sector grew significantly during the 1970s and many other occupations became indirectly subsidised by the state in its attempt to counter the activities of the IRA. The creation of a heavily subsidised middle class, with a level of disposable income significantly higher than its counterpart in other regions of the UK, gave further impetus to a new urban policy. The shifts in employment patterns in Belfast are illustrated in Table 6.1. The percentage employed in manufacturing declined from 43 per cent in 1961 to 15 per cent in 1991. Employment in services rose during the same period from 48 per cent to 80 per cent of total employment.

Although this process of labour market restructuring is not unique to Belfast, there are social and political implications involved. Protestant working-class communities were characterised by male skilled labour concentrated in heavy industry. With the decline of these industries the traditional economic and social divergence between Catholic and Protestant sections of the working class began to narrow, bringing about (at least in the west of the city) an 'equality in misery' (Table 6.2). Protestant male unemployment rose disproportionately in the northwest of the city, a situation which further discouraged labour market participation. The demise of traditional sources of male employment presents families with three options: relocation beyond the city boundary in pursuit of work, dependence upon the female members of the household for income, or welfare. Many have opted for the latter by simply dropping out of the labour market.

Table 6.1 Employment in Belfast (1961–91)

Sector	*1961*	*1971*	*1981*	*1991*
Manufacturing	76639	63257	41871	22242
Services	85073	109515	124253	132740
of which public administration and defence	8962	10949	91907	22840
TOTAL	176155	189194	174217	162295

Sources: Census of Population, 1961, 1971; Census of Employment, 1981, 1991.

Table 6.2 Labour Market Participation Rates by Gender and Marital Status (% share)

Area	*Males 1981*	*Males 1991*	*Females 1981*	*Females 1991*	*Married Females 1981*	*Married Females 1991*
Protestant northwest	76.2	66.4	42.9	39.9	43.0	43.0
Catholic northwest	78.8	70.8	43.8	42.0	36.8	41.4
Mixed north	76.1	70.9	45.0	46.8	46.5	52.0
Mixed southeast	74.1	69.5	43.5	46.0	44.4	50.1
Belfast	75.9	69.5	43.6	44.0	42.6	46.7

Source: Census of Population, 1981, 1991.

Spatial Transformation and Social Division

This is not to say there are no new opportunities for jobs at all in the city. Married women have been able to increase their presence in the labour market, and the city's southeast has become home to the new urban elite which has benefited from economic restructuring and decided, at least temporarily, to stay in the city. Redeveloping the city centre into a shopping emporium, through targeting the upper- and middle-class consumer, had the unexpected effect of creating new part-time and 'female' jobs for members of the same social classes. The second manifestation of the malfunctioning of governance was the reshaping of the urban class structure by enforcing elements of post-modernist city centre redevelopment. In effect, this benefited the already better-off, thus perpetuating the spatial pattern of inequality in the city. In addition, as shown in Table 6.3, the structural reconstruction of the city has over the past 20 years increased the number (and proportion) of jobs in the city taken by non- or ex-residents, where the proportion of residents in employment outside the city has remained largely unchanged. As shown in Table 6.3 the 15.5 per cent growth in employment held by those living outside Belfast Urban Area (BUA) has been more significant than the 0.3 per cent growth in employment of BUA residents outside the BUA. As such the dramatic restructuring of the labour market has negatively affected large sections of the BUA population (Teague, 1993b).

Table 6.3 Residence and Workplace (% share)

Year	*% of workers in BUA resident outside BUA area*	*% of BUA residents working outside BUA area*
1971	37.4	14.8
1981	43.9	10.9
1991	52.9	15.1

Source: Census of Population 1971, 1981, 1991.

The industrial working class has been decimated, the number of the long-term unemployed has increased dramatically and working-class women are being progressively squeezed out of the labour market. Yet, for some, structural change has produced new opportunities on the job market. The reshaping of the pattern of spatial segregation in the city over the last two decades has produced a concentration of a section of the Catholic service class in south Belfast. A proportion of this group is the product of upward mobility from the traditional Catholic area of west Belfast.

South Belfast has traditionally been a bastion of the Protestant bourgeoisie but has undergone a significant transformation over the last decade. The rising number of Catholics in the state and service sector can be attributed to a number of causes such as their preference for a humanities-oriented education and the effects of fair employment legislation. The growth in Catholic white collar employment due to the group's humanities-based education is somehow ironic, as ten years earlier, before the complete collapse of manufacturing, the employment shortfall endured by Catholics was continually related to their choice of 'wrong' subjects in the arts and social sciences (Miller et al., 1987). Today, south Belfast is largely Catholic and has the highest per capita income in the city.[5] For probably the first time in Belfast's history, Catholics in employment can claim higher personal income than Protestants, including higher than of those Protestants living in the traditionally prosperous east of Belfast. This reality co-exists with an overall Catholic unemployment rate twice as high as among Protestants. Yet, within the city's south, Protestants who just one or two decades ago represented the rich and established citizens of that part of town, now constitute the low income (and unemployed) class. The Catholic poor, on the other hand, have been further marginalised into the west, with two Catholic working-class enclaves also in the inner city south and east.[6]

Conclusion

Consensus and leadership are key ingredients to successful economic regeneration (Portz, 1993). In Belfast, the central state has provided leadership which, because of its sectarian legacy and the consequent segmentation of the labour market, the private sector was unable to offer. In more recent years, the central state has entered a coalition with the private sector. Paradoxically, this coalition had only become possible after the near (but literal) destruction of the urban retail sector, a process which was counter to the capitalist logic of development prevailing at the time, and subsequently successfully overcome. However, the state's failure to engage industry outside the retail and property sectors to contribute actively to economic regeneration was as much a crucial element in this process of coalition building as was the capability of the urban retail sector to organise.

State policy has consequently overdetermined both the process of economic change and the consequent changes in the class structure. The integration of a large section of the middle class into state subsidised activities concerned with the management of conflict has tended to polarise the class system, both in spatial and political terms. Long-term unemployment has increased the size of those marginalised groups (both Catholic and Protestant) dependent upon welfare for their existence in areas of the city where male unemployment rates can reach 60 per cent. For instance, in the Lower Falls area an unemployment rate of 49.3

per cent breaks down into a female rate of 37 per cent and a male rate of 58 per cent. State policy and intervention has skewed the class and occupation structure towards the state and service sector, the members of which are both employed in, and consumers of, revamped retail and service sectors. In effect, over the last ten years, the gap between those in secure employment and the rest of the population has widened with diminishing chances for the latter group while the former has gained greater access to employment. One index of this is the rising participation of married females – from the better-off sections of the population – in the labour force.

A central argument of this chapter is that the state, in its determination to fight 'terrorism' both directly and through the management of sectarian social relations, created a public sector dominated economy and artificially skewed the class structure towards a service class. This, combined with the collapse of manufacturing industry, has left vast areas of the city of Belfast dependent upon welfare as the state turned to recreating the city core as an arena of conspicuous consumption for those fortunate enough to be able to afford it. Neither the state organisations, whose functional compartmentalisation was not overcome by greater coordination and cooperation,[7] nor the private sector have been capable of providing the impetus for a successful redressing of social inequality in the city. Urban and economic policy are now under review in Northern Ireland. The difficulty encountered by the state in progressing on this issue is symptomatic of the apparatus' failure to regulate effectively the economy with more than just immediate short-term gains in mind.

Notes

1. These rules were, of course, not agreed on a democratic basis but rest upon a pragmatic acceptance by the minority that the public sphere would be organised by the Unionists around a Protestant and British ethos. The symbolism of such public spaces was, and to a large extent still is, exclusionary and triumphalist.
2. This type of urban politics was not unique to Northern Ireland. For instance, the politics of cooption was a feature of the German state's response to the urban unrest of the 1970s (Mayer, 1989).
3. The aerospace and weapons manufacturer Shorts was taken over by the Canadian company Bombardier; the Harland and

Wolff shipyard by Olsen; and Mackie's, the textile machinery manufacturer, is now part of the US firm Lummus-Mackie.

4. The policy of 'normalisation' consisted of four elements: giving priority to the police rather than to the British Army in the war against the IRA; the use of the 'normal' legal system to try and convict those suspected of terrorist-type offences; the elimination of special privileges within the prison system; and a general attempt to portray the conflict as a limited one without popular support.
5. The average Protestant income in Northern Ireland remains higher than that of Catholics (PPRU, 1993). The narrowing of the gap within Belfast is not just a result of Catholics entering higher income occupations but also of Protestants leaving to live outside the city limits.
6. Both Catholic enclaves are included in Table 6.2, in the respective sub-areas.
7. It has recently been argued that 'progress has been made with coordinating machinery at the top within the Northern Ireland Office and at the bottom through Belfast Action Teams ... but better coordination at the middle level may be required' (Birrell et al., 1993, p. 54).

7

(In)dependence, Development, and the Colonial Legacy in Comtemporary Irish Identity

LIAM GREENSLADE

I have a work by the Clare artist Mike Fitzpatrick, who exhibited in Belfast in 1993, entitled 'Gan Teanga IV'. It consists of an iconic representation of the island of Ireland in verdigris metal, set back about two inches into a frame composed from a bundle of copies of the Birmingham *Evening Mail*. The newspapers and the island are themselves enclosed in a rusty sealed metal cage. Protruding from the cage and visibly located between its bars and the island icon is a medical instrument formerly used in tracheotomy operations. The silver tube, which would be inserted in the patient's throat, and the metal plate that would hold it in place, emerge from the cage level with the location of the border between Northern Ireland and the Irish Republic. The newspaper headline, which begins in the foreground and continues into background, reads 'IRA GANG DIE IN SHOOTOUT'. The story reports the killing of four men in an attack on Coalisland RUC station in February 1992.

Whilst I have no wish to burden this work with meanings which the artist may have intended, I feel that it expresses at many levels both the obvious and less obvious ways in which the development of Ireland, both economically and culturally, has been constrained by the cage of colonialism. A cage which may be rusty, but is no less enclosing for that. Furthermore, the rustiness of the bars allows a dual signification: the temporal length of confinement and the possibility of its final erosion and removal. The emergence of the tracheotome from the anthropomorphised 'throat' of the island adds a further dimension to the imagery of constraint. It signifies, in my opinion, not merely the absence of a voice, the crude silencing of the gag, but its diversion, both literally and metamorphically into other channels. It is important that we interrogate some of these constraints and the ways in which they emerge as part of everyday subjective practice and understanding, what Marx and Engels (1970, p. 48) have called the 'active life-process'. My argument is premised on the view that the systematic underdevelopment of the Irish economy which characterised British colonial rule and the political, ideological and social processes which accompanied it have continued to exert an effect upon contemporary Irish lives, through directly affecting the manner in which people on the island of Ireland understand themselves and their situation and develop strategies to deal with their personal and collective identities (Crotty, 1986; Kennedy et al., 1988).

This chapter argues that the long-term, overdetermining effects of colonialism have created a set of pathological double binds which have been incorporated into the political unconscious of Irish culture and identity, and which in turn feed back into the conscious efforts of people on the island of Ireland to engage with their history and its consequences (Jameson, 1981). Economic underdevelopment of a kind specific to Ireland in its historical position as the 'first capitalist colony' is a significant causal factor in this process but it is not the only part (Crotty, 1986). My concern is with the kind of socio-psychological underdevelopment characteristic of colonial and post-colonial cultures best described in the works of Fanon (1967) and Memmi (1965), and the impact that it has on the ways in which Irish people come to terms with and attempt to change their relationship to their history. My aim is to examine some of the 'voices' which emerge from Fitzpatrick's tracheotome, place them in the context of this kind of underdevelopment and recast them in a way which shows the commonality of historical and economic experience underlying them.

Double Binds and Behavioural Ideologies

A concept that will crop up throughout this chapter is that of the 'double bind'. My use of it in this context derives from the work of Wilden (1987a, 1987b). He defines it as follows:

> A true double bind ... requires a choice between (at least) two states or situations that are so equally valued and so equally insufficient that a self-perpetuating oscillation is set up by any act of choice between them ... The necessity of choosing is not, however, imposed by the double bind as such; it is imposed by the context that constrains one's relative freedom of response, one's relative diversity of behaviour and communication, in

> dealing with the double bind ... what produces the oscillation in a binary double bind is that one is required to choose to satisfy *either* condition A *or* condition B within a set of metaconditions that can only be satisfied by *both* A *and* B. (1987a, pp. 96–7, emphasis in original)

What is at stake in the double bind and what produces its pathologies, as Bateson (1973) has argued, is not merely choice, but rather it is survival; physical, psychological, cultural, social, and/or economic. Schizophrenia is one kind of response to a double bind. The recognition that all communication is potentially pathological results in a total refusal to communicate with tragic consequences for the person making the recognition. The schizophrenic 'knows' there is something wrong but is prevented from knowing 'where' it is wrong and can find no way of escaping the constraints of the context except through psychological withdrawal in a refusal to play the game of normal behaviour and communication (Greenslade, 1991). The schizophrenic double bind is tragic because in making the choice not to communicate, the schizophrenic ignores the fact that one of the metaconditions in a human context is that one cannot not communicate (Bateson, 1973). Transcending double binds requires both a recognition of the nature of the choices and the metaconditions or contexts in which they occur. The schizophrenic responds 'appropriately' to the former, but is unable to do anything about the latter.

A second concept informing this paper is that of 'behavioural ideology' furnished by the Soviet semiotician Volosinov (1973). Behavioural ideologies constitute the terrain where people act through and mediate the relationships between real and imaginary contexts, between official ideological versions of reality and reality as it is experienced. The 'official' ideologies of a given society reflect in large part the world outlook, morality, and historical development of the groups which dominate it. In a class society, needless to say, there is a constant struggle to maintain ideological hegemony. That is, to legitimise the world view of the dominant group. It is in the realm of behavioural, 'unofficial' ideology that the consequences of this struggle come to be recognised and acted against.

Unlike official ideologies which seek to normalise, legitimise and remove the conflictual aspects of experience, behavioural ideologies are highly attuned to the gap between life as experienced and official interpretations of that experience. Behavioural ideologies should not be understood as free-floating sets of ideas, but rather as the concrete actions of human beings caught in particular sets of material circumstances, which for better or worse they must find some way of surviving. In double bound environments, such as the kind which induce schizophrenia, behavioural ideologies pointedly reflect the extremes of survival which are at stake. The official ideologies in societies based on class, patriarchy or other forms of oppression are ultimately legitimised by the threat of violence, real or symbolic. Double binds in these settings often concern matters of life or death.

For Irish people, the significant context is their history of colonialism and the relative economic and political underdevelopment that resulted from it. The double binds of interest here emerge primarily at the cultural and political level. These are articulated as a series of behavioural ideologies which appear in a binary either/or form: nationalism/unionism (or loyalism), emigration/settlement, madness/sanity, Catholic/Protestant, and so forth. These articulations in turn become constituents in imaginary individual and cultural identities and find their symbolic expression in practical social relations which create the reality of existence for people in Ireland today. Within these 'choices', formed out of a distinct set of historical experiences but which fail to recognise the real nature of those experiences and their consequences, there is little or no middle ground which individuals or communities can safely inhabit.

The examination of double binds and their relationship to Irish identity is here centred upon an analysis of the surrounding and co-existing (and competing) discourses of nationalism. It shall be argued that these binds represent, in their different ways, coherent, if conflictual, responses to an incoherent and inappropriate reality, rather than vice versa, as they are often represented and interpreted. These nationalisms represent historically double bound responses to the lasting effects of colonialism on social relationships and ways of 'thinking about the world' in modern Ireland. They are imaginary representations of states of affairs which have very real consequences, not least of which are their paralysing implications for economic, social and cultural development within the island of Ireland as a whole.

'Development' in this context therefore means more than the ability to generate economic wealth by becoming a 'modern' European bourgeois state, achieved through emulating the model of the oppressor. It means going beyond the inherent limitations of that socio-economic structure and creating an environment freed from the chains of its colonial history in which people can develop according to their real needs and circumstances.

The Basis of the Colonised Consciousness

Prior to independence, as both Fanon (1967) and Memmi (1965) have noted, the relationship between coloniser and colonised is based on an imaginary construction in which the latter is held to be dependent on the former. Sustained by the colonist's control of the economic and ideological environment of the colony, this inversion imbues the psychological life of the colonised with extraordinarily neurotic identifications and misrecognitions (Fanon, 1970; Kirby, 1988). Among the principal features of this inversion is the so-called 'dependency complex' of colonised people (Mannoni, 1964). Psycho-socially, this manifests itself in a need to validate themselves and their culture in the eyes of the colonist, to prove their worth as human beings in terms set by the colonial order. This activity is purely imaginary, since in the real terms of the colonial relationship, the native will always be the native, in other words a primitive inferior to, or shoddy copy of, the colonist. That is a simple consequence of the way in which the colonial relationship is set up as a historical fact. After independence, after the colonist has departed, a new 'dependency complex' which is no longer imaginary begins to assert itself; the economic dependency of the former colony on the so-called mother country, for its markets, exports and livelihoods. Now, the interaction between native and coloniser takes on a new form in which the coloniser is merely an absence, or in the specific case of Ireland a partial absence.

To the extent that the colonial structures are not themselves fundamentally revised in the post-colonial period and the basic economic relationships both within the post-colonial society and between it and the former colonial power are maintained, then a rupture occurs in the fabric of experience. So long as colonial structures still exert themselves then their most pernicious socio-psychological side-effects continue even though the rational and intelligible means for articulating and understanding them have physically departed. If we are unable to manage our economy, it must be our fault. If our culture seems contradictory and riven by conflict, then who can we blame but ourselves. The alternative is to engage in denial; to ignore the economic facts and depend on emigration to keep the jobless figures down, to emphasise the positive and harmonious aspects while ignoring the oppressive ones, and so on.

In short, the colonial legacy creates a society of begrudgers. Within such societies victims make victims out of each other as the struggle to break the double binds of colonialism continues. With each individual or group passing on its structured and internalised inferiority on to other groups within the system; men on to women, native bourgeoisie on to native proletariat, abandoned settler on to native. As Lee has put it in the case of Ireland, social relations become characterised '... by a cosmic displacement of bilious resentment' (1989, p. 647). At the societal level, the desire for recognition by the absent (colonial) 'other', the desire to exhibit equal mastery and competency over history and one's own affairs becomes central (Kenny, 1985). As a result, recognition is gained at the expense of others within the post-colonial society. In particular those institutions which, during the time of the colonist's presence formed the principal sites of resistance and succour (e.g. the family, tribe, indigenous religion, and so forth), change their function in such societies. As they become drawn into official ideological purview of the post-colonial state, their revolutionary or emancipatory components ossify, they become conservative and ridden by internal conflicts derived from the contradiction between their revolutionary past and their normalising function in the present.

One feature which may contribute to this ossification in the post-colonial world is the divorce between material bases of economic and cultural power which the colonial bestows upon the native state. As Fanon (1967) has observed, the post-colonial native bourgeoisie to the extent that it is a relatively underdeveloped group, both in terms of numbers and outlook, is incapable of doing away with the material legacy of colonialism and creating out of its own resources a 'modern' nation. Its model of development and its standards of legitimacy are set by the colonist, however inappropriate they might be to goals of national liberation. In short, with its limited resources the nationalist middle class disregards the real needs of the people and strives to consolidate its hold over the space vacated by the coloniser. In Fanon's words it:

> ... discovers its historic mission: that of intermediary ... and it will play its part without any complexes in a most dignified manner. Seen through its eyes, its mission has nothing to do with transforming the nation; it consists prosaically, of being

> the transmission line between the nation and capitalism ... (1967, p. 122)

Nonetheless, this class holds in its hands control of the material economy of the new state, such as it is. Legitimising its control, however much at variance its interests may be from those of the people as a whole, requires that it develops the means to neutralise the revolutionary tendencies who would wish to continue the removal of the colonist's hand in the destiny of the new state. They cannot so readily use the mechanisms of coercion available to the colonist to accomplish this and so greater effort is expended in the domain of culture and ideology. Central to this coercion or incitement are the concepts of 'nation' and 'national identity'.

Both north and south of the border, this concept of 'national identity', a hand-me-down from British imperialism, has been utilised as an excuse in the furtherance of oppression, economic or political, as a means of inciting oppressed people to act against their own long range interest. An idea of 'nation' is drawn upon constantly to shore up the bankrupt actions of a national bourgeoisie whose main goal is to maximise their profits and further their privileges. It ultimately results in little more than a form of consciousness that reflects the needs of a tiny and unrepresentative group within the post-colonial society as a whole. The reality of experience for those outside of this group becomes increasingly marginalised as the idea of the nation, the horizontal community, articulated according to the needs of the post-colonial bourgeoisie, becomes crystallised into an official ideology. The power of this articulation process is strikingly exhibited in the case of tourism. Ultimately everything within the post-colonial culture becomes a marketable commodity, geared to making profit for the national bourgeoisie, even the backwardness and underdevelopment of the country itself. The promotion of tourism as a means of generating a livelihood for a significant proportion of the population is symptomatic of the nationalist bourgeoisie's ability to manipulate reality for their own ends. Inherently incapable of producing the nation that they promised, they extract capital from the idea of the nation itself.

The promotion of tourism as a national 'industry' is a chilling reminder of the economic reality and relationships in which the post-colonial nation finds itself. No other industry illustrates so well the real relationship of dependency between those who manage the economy and those who truly determine its fate. Apart from being a short-term answer to a long-range problem, tourism transforms the people who have to service such an economy into little more than servants whose livelihood is wholly dependent on the whims and the economies of non-nationals. It transforms local culture and environment into a 'cash-crop' and reinforces the relationship of inferiority/superiority between representatives of the developing and the developed countries. That tourism can be seen widely as a meaningful contributor to future development, to the resolution of unemployment and emigration in Ireland, is a tribute to the way in which the post-colonial bourgeoisie have harnessed ideology to their own economic interest.

Inventing the Nation

The relative weakness of the national bourgeoisie in the post-colonial state, and the contradictions between class interest and national aspiration, open up an opportunity to another group: the nationalist intelligentsia. This group is, by the very nature of the colonial project, far more developed and extensive (Anderson, 1989). It falls to them to play a significant role in the development of the post-colonial nation in outlining the boundaries of national identity and culture, in determining what is and what is not legitimate, or merely intelligible, within those boundaries and amongst the people of the post-colonial state, and in furnishing the means by which the mass of people may articulate the relationship between lived experience and material reality.

The central role of the native intelligentsia in the rise of nationalism is marked thus by a paradox. Their conception of the nation, what it is and what it could be, is based on the model of the conqueror, while the materials from which they must build this nation, the national culture and economy on which it must grow have, throughout their colonial history and training, been painted as the quintessence of backwardness and primitive barbarism (Fanon, 1967; Memmi, 1965). The native intelligentsia has to find some way of reconciling this contradiction before it can begin the task which the nationalist bourgeoisie has laid before it.

The current debate in Irish historiography between revisionism and nationalism is a good example of how this contradiction is being worked out within Ireland. The debate is one in which the forces at play are concerned with the interpretation of the historical experience of the Irish people in which ironically the actuality of that experience is secondary. Manifesting itself crudely in a contest between 'nationalist' and 'revisionist' programmes of public history, this struggle has resulted in historiography, which is central in the role of constructing national identities and origin myths, alternating schizophrenically between two kinds of public history (Bradshaw, 1992). The nationalist historiography developed throughout the nineteenth century sought to unify Irish people around the struggle of native against foreign invader, the Gael against the Gall. Its narratives were constructed to imbue national identity with a strongly Catholic dimension. Their revisionist counterparts who, for a variety of reasons, were to dominate the field for many years after partition sought the removal of these 'myths'. In neither case was a history produced in which anyone but historians themselves could place any faith. The reason for this is perhaps more obvious than one would think, given the complexity of the ways in which it comes to be articulated. It is because the version of nationalism developed in Ireland during the nineteenth century and articulated ever since is typical, in both form and function, of the nationalisms developed elsewhere in Europe during that period. It is what Anderson (1989) has termed 'official'. That is, it emanates from the state and exists to preserve and protect the interests of the state first and foremost. As Anderson puts it:

> At a less obvious level, successful revolutionaries also inherit the wiring of the old state ... Like the complex electrical system in any large mansion when the owner has fled, the state awaits the new owner's hand at the switch to be very much its brilliant old self again. (1989, p. 160)

In short, and echoing Connolly's remarks (1973) on the hoisting of the green flag over Dublin, it is the very structure of the post-colonial state which is at the heart of the dilemma of the native intellectual, since their very role is created by its existence and they exist implicitly to serve it. Symptomatic of native intelligentsia generally, in their capacity as functional intellectuals, Irish historians have found themselves unable to manoeuvre around the conflicting 'choices' built into the historical wiring of the post-colonial state. Native intellectuals in this situation exist in an imaginary relationship to their environment where their function in articulating the dimensions and boundaries of the post-colonial nation are inextricably tied to the ultimately conservative nature of the state structure itself. In this context, a confusion arises between the idea of the nation, a real or imagined community of individuals sharing some common attributes or experiences, and the idea of the state, a political and legal entity with powers to coerce its citizens.

North of the border, different, if complementary, contradictions arise. Here, the goal is less to present the contradictions of the emergent nation in a positive light, to diminish or promote the past according to views which, though sincere, are based on a contradictory understanding of the intellectuals' historical and ideological function. In the North, the intellectual project has been one based on silence. Moreover, it has been centred upon a detachment from the materiality of the situation coupled with a painful awareness of the significance of intellectual activity on the one hand and the consequences of taking a position on the other (Fennell, 1993).

The Impossible Union: Between Nation and State

Much of the on-going debate and discussion surrounding 'Irish identity' stems ultimately from contradictory and somewhat confusing notions of nation and state (e.g. Tovery et al., 1989). If, as Anderson (1989) observes, the nation is an imagined community, then the post-colonial state, to the extent that it has failed to eradicate the oppressive institutions and social relations of the colonial period, is an imaginary community. A community whose subjects are required constantly to shore themselves up against the contradictions brought about by a liberation which did not entail emancipation, independence which did not entail autonomy, and empowerment which did not entail security, economic or psychic. The conflictual nature of the state–nation relationship as it occurs on the island of Ireland, although rooted in the political economy, finds itself most strongly articulated in the intellectual output of the post-colonial community as much by what it elides as by what it concentrates upon. Thus we find a clear and obvious divide between intellectuals north and south of the border. In the North where, for nationalists at least, the state has always been the primary problematic entity, a focal machinery of division and repression, a whole body of literature has appeared analysing its structure, function, and implications (Bew et al., 1980; De Paor, 1970; Farrell, 1976; O'Dowd et al., 1980).

The reverse is true for the modern Republic of Ireland. As Lee (1989) has pointed out, there has been almost no systematic investigation of the Irish state since partition. Intellectuals in the South have instead tended to focus less upon the state itself, and more upon the characteristics of the nation and national identity, its people, and its economy, neglecting or avoiding the political structure and its characteristics. Thus we will find numerous texts on Irish identity, on rural and urban Ireland, on the success and failure of the economy and its various governments, on religion, on culture, and so forth, but little in the way of a rigorous attempt to show how these things relate to each other and are mediated by the structure of the state itself. The relative levels of interest and neglect on either side of the border can be linked to the day-to-day experience of the state–nation relationship as it has been historically constructed. In the South, the burgeoning problem has always been one of reconciling the needs of the state with the characteristics and aspirations of the nation.

In the North, because the state was constructed to embody a concrete set of economic and social privileges based around religious practice, an answer to that question was always available, if only in its material implications. The answer was always and inescapably 'Catholic' or 'Protestant' (and by no means necessarily 'nationalist' or 'loyalist'). What was and remains problematic was the nature of the entity which furnished the answer. The colonial position of the majority could be resolved by their subsumption within the British state. For them, national identity was not a problem, as such. The practical problem was how that state should function in its self-preservation. For the minority, the problem was one of survival within its territorial boundaries, given that the neighbouring state, if not the nation, had all but abandoned them.

Therefore a situation has arisen where, for intellectuals at least, Northern Ireland represents a state without a nation and the Republic of Ireland a nation without a state, insofar as the first term in each equation can be regarded as unproblematic. In both places, to choose one or the other, or to reject both, is to enter into conflict with one's self or with one's community. But every day necessitates that choices be made. The relationship between state and nation, as reflected in this discussion of intellectual production, leads us back to where we began, with the images of constraint and reality reflected in the work by Mike Fitzpatrick.

Imagined States: Nationalism(s) in Modern Ireland

As noted above the contrast between North and South in the present context can be summed up readily. If the South is a nation without a state, then the North is a state without a nation.

Following Anderson (1989), we can see at least in the modern period of state formation the reality of the state entails the construction of an imagined community of the nation, if only as a part of the ideological project of the nationalist bourgeoisie in furthering their economic ends. What we see in late twentieth-century Ireland is the working out of the unresolved dimensions of the history which has led to this situation. On both sides of the border it is as if history has finally caught up with reality.

From the moment of partition onwards, people both north and south of the border have effectively been side-tracked from history by those who have sought to profit from the colonist's withdrawal. Their voices have been constrained and their actions limited by official ideologies which sought to transform history, the ongoing and active engagement with the present, into a dead and buried past. Unfortunately, it is a past which will not lie down. But the responses which have emerged to it reflect its unresolved tragedies.

So we see in the Republic levels of emigration unparalleled since the 1950s, for quitting the context is an effective if short-term solution to the problem of the double bind. Amongst those who stay we find a sense of bewilderment and quasi-mysticism, unthought of conflict between tradition and modernity, and the growing recognition of the division between the 'green Tory' nationalism of Dublin 4 and the nation itself (Fennell, 1993; Waters, 1991). As O'Toole put it, by the 1980s:

> The sense of Ireland as an invention, a fantasy, as something up for grabs and needing to be refashioned every time a speech was made or a painting begun, became overwhelming ... events were unbelievable even though they had happened, anything could mean everything, and everything was unprecedented ... Tradition could only be used ironically. (1990, pp. 12–13)

In short, the nationalism which was called upon to justify and exonerate the nature and failure of the state was simply ceasing to function and could no longer be held in place by foreign loans or the mass haemorrhage of its people. For the people as a whole, the traditional mythology of de Valera simply could no longer heal the cracks in the modern reality which may be seen as an inevitable outcome of the short-term strategies adopted by the Irish bourgeoisie. In such a situation people did what they could; for some it was emigration, for others it was millenarianism in the form of moving statues. In either case, a practical attempt to answer the painful question of identity is foregone.

In the North, parallel developments have occurred as the dominant caste found its economic base under growing scrutiny from the new conservatism in Britain (Rowthorn and Wayne, 1988). Here, people found themselves caught between the thrusting modernity which had characterised the Protestant state, symbolised in its imagery of King Billy, and the Boyne and its crushing traditionalism and resistance to change within its own borders, symbolised this time in the siege of Derry. In this society, people have entered into the process of articulating a unique national identity for themselves which does not rely, for it can no longer so easily do so, on their claims to 'Britishness'. There is a long step from Jim Wells' confident assertion of his Britishness in 1985 (cited in O'Toole, 1990, p. 62) to Ian Paisley Jr's assertion of his (Ulster) Irishness in the pages of the *Irish Post* in 1992 (cited in Foley, 1992, p. 5).

While stepping up the level of sectarian warfare, loyalists have begun to appropriate the mythology of old, Celtic Ireland as a means to generating their own myth of origin, its own imagined community (McAuley, 1991). The same CúChullain, whose statue stands in the General Post Office in Dublin, the scene of the birth of the modern Irish Republic, has been drawn upon as a symbol of loyalist indefatigability. Meanwhile the state which had preserved its rights and privileges has begun to wither away beneath it. The withering away of the state is most marked by the suspicion which clearly exits between loyalist activists and their political representatives (Anon, 1984; McAuley, 1991). The people, whose right to exert their 'Britishness' in triumphalist parades, whose right to display its emblems is enshrined in the law, now openly express their fears about the role of the state in committing 'cultural genocide' against them in such programmes as Education for Mutual Understanding (Anon, 1990, p. 1). Ever more so the siege was replacing the Boyne as principal signifier of loyalist ideology. Only now its assailants came not merely from within the territory (i.e. Catholics and nationalists) but also from without (i.e. Westminster). The Union, which defined the state but obviated the nation, has ceased to render the world intelligible. There is a sense of betrayal within the community as that which was 'solid melts into air' (Shriver, 1993).

One symptom of the growing recognition of the willingness of the British to forego its support for the Northern Ireland state and the divorce between the grassroots of loyalism and its official ideologies is the bestowing of a class dimension, in contrast to the 'pan-Protestant' character of traditional Unionism and loyalism, succinctly expressed by Cameron as follows:

> Protestants who cannot see beyond the Union tend to be, though not exclusively so, upper and middle class. People who are generally '*well off*' financially and who have cultivated tendencies towards the lifestyle they perceive to be the norm of their peers and 'betters' on mainland (*sic*) Britain. (1993, p. 130, italics in original)

What all this amounts to, in short, is a realisation that the colonial state which enabled them to go for so long without developing a nationalism of the kind described by Anderson (1989) was revealing its true bankruptcy insofar as many of its supporters, both active and passive, were concerned. A realisation that they had become, in effect, subject to the forces of history rather than subjects of history had begun to dawn. Reality has, in a sense, overtaken the tradition of the 'pan-Protestant' ascendant experience and this is reflected in the attempt to invent a national identity which parallels that of their Catholic neighbours.

The third group caught up in this situation, the diverse Republican/nationalist Catholic communities of Northern Ireland find themselves caught in an analogous dilemma. Through no fault of their own they have been locked into competing senses of tradition and modernity, most pointed in the conflict of ideas and practices making up constitutional nationalism and revolutionary republicanism. As a materially oppressed group within Northern Ireland, their situation is perhaps the most poignant of all, for like all the oppressed and disempowered, the exercise of such power as they possess becomes fraught with contradiction. Their experience of systematic violence on a day-to-day basis generates at one and the same time the realisation that violence is one medium of communication understood by the system which positions and acts upon them and also a recognition of the implications of using violence for their own ends (Connolly, 1973; Fanon, 1967). The former recognition recommends the use of physical force, the latter refutes it as anathema at its worst or relegates it to a reluctantly adopted component of the struggle at best. Linked to this is a set of tensions between the experience of themselves as 'oppressed' on the one hand and as 'revolutionary' on the other, in the widest possible sense of both these terms, and the way in which these sensibilities are imbricated in the contradictory tradition of Irish nationalism in its conservative (i.e. Gaelic/Catholic) and its radical (internationalist/secular) manifestations (Adams, 1986).

Nonetheless, what emerges from them is the necessary understanding of the limited possibility of realising Anderson's (1989) 'official' (i.e. state) nationalism in the material context of the late twentieth-century Northern Ireland. This understanding takes on its positive form in the development of the class-based, populist approaches which emerged with a renewed force during the 1980s arguing for a genuine attainment of social justice and independence. Its negative form, which also became apparent in the same period, was the use of nationalism for reformist ends, as a means of squeezing concessions from the state without fundamentally challenging its form (Patterson, 1989).

Conclusion

If the foregoing sketches teach us anything, it is that there are inherent limitations and pernicious consequences attached to inventing a national identity or articulating a nationalism based on metropolitan lines. It is particularly inappropriate in a terrain which has experienced long-term colonialism and whose economy is still locked into a dependent relationship with the metropolitan powers. A project of national liberation is quite distinct from a struggle to replace foreign oppression with its home grown variety. We do not have to define ourselves in terms of any nationalism, except under strictly limited circumstances, nor is it in the interests of long-term survival for us to do so, if only because the idea of the nation is inherently limiting. The point is that if we are to overcome the inherent limitations of our ideas of nation and escape the cage which Fitzpatrick places around the whole of Ireland, we have to recognise its presence and understand the nature of its construction. This is merely a preface, however, to the real task of developing practices which are based on what unites us rather than on the limited understanding of what divides us and the options for change with which that presents us.

Here, I believe, is where the real prospect for development, economic or otherwise, arises. It is in disabusing ourselves of the idea of a nation which we did not ourselves develop, which has no real meaning for our experience, and which artificially and painfully constrains our ways of thinking and being in the world. Like all the machinery of bourgeois social practice, it forces us into substituting short-term benefits for long-range survival. In a country whose only real resource is its people, disaster is the inevitable result of such an exchange.

In the long term, development for the people on the island of Ireland, and for the countless members of the Irish diaspora, will truly arise only when we learn the lessons that our history teaches us, when we understand the nature of the limitations it has imposed on us, and engage an active process of changing that history to make it work for us, rather than against us. Our situation is not and can never be the same as that of the metropolitan states of Europe. That is not negotiable. But we can break out of the pernicious oscillation between unsatisfactory alternatives with which our long colonial history has presented us. If there is any conclusion to be drawn here at all, it is perhaps in the possibility of a point of departure most aptly stated by Franz Fanon:

> So, comrades, let us not pay tribute to Europe by creating states, institutions and societies which draw their inspiration from her ... For Europe, for ourselves and for humanity, comrades, we must turn over a new leaf, we must work out new concepts, and try to set afoot a new man. (1967, pp. 254–5)

8

Development Discourses: Conservative, Radical and Beyond

RONNIE MUNCK AND HONOR FAGAN

Development holds a central place in many debates but it is seldom deconstructed. It is a discourse made up of a web of key concepts which are simply taken for granted, in both its conservative and radical guises. Development is an amoeba-like concept – denoting everything and nothing – which creates a common ground for right and left to battle on. Thus, if there is a perceived impasse in development theory, this should be seen as due to the stultifying unity of the discursive field and not its regrettable fragmentation (Schuurman, 1993). We argue in this chapter that the crisis of development theory – and by implication the crisis of development perspectives in Ireland – is linked to the limitations of the modernist discourse. As we do not seek an abstract critique of existing radical debates, but a genuine transcending, we shall proceed first to catalogue the considerable achievements of this work – as exemplified in this book – in questioning the findings of conservative or 'mainstream' thinking on the development prospects of Ireland. In the course of this analysis we hope to move beyond the language of critique to a language of transformation, necessary in our view for any radical democratic vision and creation of a new Ireland.

Economic Fallacies

Virtually all the contributors to this volume would agree on the poverty of 'mainstream', conventional or conservative remedies for the crisis of development in Ireland today. Prionnsias Breathnach refers in this regard to the 'tunnel vision' characteristic of Irish economists' and their reliance on British or US 'metropolitan' models of development. For the once dominant, then defunct, now reborn modernisation or developmentalist model, there is an inexorable drive towards modernity that all nation states will equally participate in. It is not hard to show that Ireland has been largely excluded from this 'best of all possible worlds', as Rousseau would have it. For most contributors to this volume this is due to Ireland's condition of ill-defined 'peripherality'. But if this is not to be simply tautology – Ireland is excluded from the development process because it is peripheral, and Ireland is peripheral because it is excluded from the development process – more definition is needed. Douglas Hamilton refers to geographic peripherality and economic peripherality in his contribution. Considerable emphasis is laid on the role of multinational or transnational companies in constraining the development prospects of Ireland. The implicit alternative in both contributions is some form of national or 'autonomous' development model which would look 'inward' to Ireland rather than 'outward' to the world economy.

It is only recently that Mjoset (1992) has brought home to Ireland some of the advances in international development theory and research, although O'Malley's (1989) earlier work in the 'Sussex school' tradition of 'structural dependency' should also be mentioned. It is significant that Breathnach's opening contribution bases its analysis squarely on Mjoset's idea of a 'vicious circle' or underdevelopment. This refers to a process, familiar to Third World economists, in which there is a mutual negative interaction between features such as population decline, a sluggish home market, a weak national system of innovation and the threat of marginalisation from the mainstream of world economic life. Mjoset is incorrect, however, in associating 'peripheral development' with growth without development, insofar as the Latin American dependency school always recognised the possibility of dependent development and was not stagnationist. The main point, however, is well taken and it is significant that Mjoset's work should be seen as so novel in Ireland when it is only essentially an 'application' of Third World development perspectives to the Irish case. It certainly establishes fairly conclusively the weakness of the development model in Ireland, both in the past and today. O'Hearn's (1993) recent contribution to a study of global competition, Europe and Irish peripherality, should also be mentioned as part of the radical critique of complacent mainstream views in this regard.

If the radical critique of the 'mainstream' highlights dependency and the vicious circle of underdevelopment, it also, justifiably, focuses on the human costs of this seemingly impersonal process. Paul Sweeney's contribution to this volume has no problem in clearly identifying the key fundamental problem of development in Ireland as the inter-related problems of mass unemployment and emigration. There is the well-founded saying that the Southern economy is working well, pity about the people! The conservative advice that people should not 'price themselves out of jobs' is now being applied with a vengeance. In the South and the North alike, workers have consistently been told that if their wages were reduced and productivity was increased, more jobs would result. Yet while real unit labour costs have fallen consistently, the dole queues have lengthened and emigration regains its traditional role in the Irish socio-economic system. It is perhaps well to remind the Irish economists, who advocate economic policies regardless of their social impact, that their international development colleagues are increasingly being called upon to justify and apply ethical principles to the policies they advocate. As Amartya Sen, one of the foremost contemporary development economists, puts it: 'While the tendency to avoid facing foundational questions is quite common, it is more a reflection of escapism than a demonstration of uncanny wisdom' (1989, p. 772).

Virtuous Governance

If the economic fallacies of the mainstream are plain to see, we should also ask questions about the political system which allows this state of affairs to persist. In the South, for example, the *Culliton Report* (1992) put forward a quite coherent and, in its own way, radical set of proposals to overcome the development crisis. Yet, from the political arena we have witnessed a bold new departure in terms of economic policy. In the North, as Clulow and Teague (1993) argue, every level and component of the governance structure is faulty and, therefore, a serious impediment to improved economic performance. Virtuous governance can be seen as a narrow economistic concept – a sort of enabling political structure – or as a broader commitment to democracy in all spheres of social life. It is at this point that we are reminded that economics is really (or should be) about political economy. The recent history of international economics in which neo-liberal economic strategies could be advocated almost regardless of their social and political consequences has not been superseded. In Ireland it is still, however, considered 'subversive' to advocate alternative economic strategies which in any way question or undermine existing political and institutional arrangements.

One of the main manifestations of the 'democratic deficit' with regards to development in Ireland remains, we would argue, the question of partition. Even the mainstream economists reporting to the New Ireland Forum in 1984 recognised the substantial economic benefits of a reunited Ireland in terms of economies of scale and scope. In terms of the vicious circle of under-development analysed above we can, conversely, envisage a virtuous circle of development (synergy) as part of a dynamic process of Irish reunification within Europe. However, it should be mentioned that much of the current debate on a reunited Ireland has been within an economic framework, without acknowledging fully the wider political environment in which economic affairs operate. From a radical democratic perspective we need to stress the social, political and cultural divisions introduced by partition which are all, in their different ways, barriers to the harmonious development of Ireland. It is this broader democratic debate which can take us away from McGimpsey's (1993) sterile discussion on the 'economic impossibility of a united Ireland', as one recent paper put it. Equally, it should make us question the naive belief of some northern economic spokespersons – such as George Quigley – that an 'island economy' may be profitably developed in Ireland without in any way compromising existing constitutional arrangements.

It is indicative of the parochialism of much of the development debate in Ireland that there is little reference to the long-standing international discussion on the relationship between development and democracy (Sklair, 1988). Some twenty years ago this debate centred around the developmental preconditions for achieving democratic governance. More recently there has been a turn towards examining the political preconditions – such as democratic governance – for achieving genuine self-sustaining development. Yet in both trends we note normative, coercive and ultimately untenable views of democracy and development, sustaining a master narrative based on the idea of a homogeneous, universal history. Democracy has been, for too long, an abstract Western ideal inextricably bound up with a particular notion of (capitalist) development. We should instead recognise the proliferation of meanings lying behind the terms 'development' and 'democracy'. That both are floating signifiers should be both self-evident and a necessary condition in creating the terrain for an open debate on the preferred political outcome. Given the discursive centrality of both terms, these signifiers are bound to be ambiguous, and the site of important social and political practices. If the 'identity' of development and democracy is ambiguous and lacks fixity, we should not, from a radical democratic perspective, take any mainstream definitions for granted.

Radical Options

Having established the limitations of the conservative development discourse, in its economic and political aspects, the radical alternative needs to present its own options. Breathnach refers to Samir Amin's (1990) notion of 'autocratic development', Hamilton stresses the need for greater autonomy, and Walsh calls for a more radical National Development Plan. Thus the radical alternative can be said to be inward looking and state oriented. Indeed, one of the problems with the radical dependency theory since its origins was its failure to articulate clearly what non-dependent development might mean, beyond vague gestures about the need to 'delink' from the world economy. The logical corollary of autarky – basically closing economic frontiers and striving for self-sufficiency – is not only reactionary but clearly not economically viable in today's world. Any revival of 1930s de Valera-type economics in Ireland today would be, quite literally, a reactionary and chauvinist pipedream. It is only when we restrict ourselves to the self-limiting world of binary oppositions that we could oppose an outward-oriented and exploitative economic model with a simple inward-oriented model. Instead, we should perhaps be exploring – without preconceptions – which combination of viable economic measures could best meet the main social and economic needs and aspirations of the Irish people.

In development discourses as a whole we find that the state is traditionally attributed a master role as conductor and conduit of development. More recently we have witnessed a new orthodoxy in which the state is perceived and presented as the main obstacle to development (Colcough and Manor, 1993). Again, as in the democracy and development debate, we see the debilitating presence of binary opposites. It is simply not enough for radicals today to portray increased state intervention as the path to true development. Whatever the limitations of the neo-liberal recipes and the uncritical celebration of the market, we cannot ignore the well-founded criticism of state capitalism and the associated strategies of social engineering. The new liberalism and state capitalism alike share an economism which sees economic growth as the centrepiece of social change and a teleology which assumes a goal-oriented development process. It might be useful for the Irish democratic development debate to look at current radical South African alternative economic discourse. With regard to the role of the state, the recent Macro Economic Research Group report *Making Democracy Work* (1993) contains an apparently 'conservative' call for 'a slim state, disciplined by mechanisms which provide incentives for efficiency and for monitoring of performance' (1993, p. 3). Only a blinkered and dogmatic view of social change could dismiss this realistic appraisal out of hand.

Paul Sweeney's contribution to this volume is geared specifically to providing a trade union response to the development crisis in Ireland. While sympathetic to any rejection of knee-jerk reactions towards capitalist proposals, we remain sceptical of the extent to which some Irish trade unionists have accepted policies such as HRM which are central to the neo-Fordist enterprise. It is not an effective counter-discourse to hegemonic economic thinking just to demand that the profits of technological change be shared more equitably. Other trade unionists have argued that a progressive economic alternative 'demands not only more resources, reorganisation of the development effort, more popular participation and public accountability, but also a conceptual rethinking of economic priorities' (Freeman et al., 1987). The last point can be related to the ever more pressing concern with the environment and the extent to which 'malestream' economic development conspires against the interests of women (Moser, 1989). An alternative economic strategy in Ireland will not materialise, in our mind, without a considerable increase in popular participation. To be more specific, a democratic economic policy in Ireland can only emerge in the context of a peace settlement leading to the creation of an all-Ireland democracy, where participation might increase in all spheres of social life, including economic policy making.

Radical Fallacies

It is now generally recognised that radical development theory has been in some sort of impasse over the last few years. This is not, however, self-evident from the contributions to this volume which assume a coherent and viable alternative to the current conservative development nostrums. It may be useful to examine this question in terms of what has been seen as one of the central manifestations of the modernist discourse, namely logocentrism. The concept refers to a tendency to impose hierarchy on uncritically accepted dichotomies between, for example, men and women, modern and traditional, or North and South. The first term is seen as a sovereign subject, an invariable presence needing no explanation, whereas the second is seen simply as derivative and defined solely in relation to the first. As Manzo (1991) points out, the concept of logocentrism is important to this discussion because, 'it demonstrates how even the most radically critical discourse easily slips into the form, the logic, and even the implicit postulations of precisely what it seeks to contest, for it can never completely step outside a heritage from which it must borrow its tools ...' (1991, p. 8). So pervasive is the logocentric mode within development studies, that any challenge to the dominant assumption of economic growth can hardly be entertained.

It is somewhat overgeneralised but arguable to state that the radical dependency model is, in fact, just a form of economic nationalism. The dependency approach took for granted that 'development' meant what had happened in Britain or the US. In Derrida's terms these experiences belonged to the realm of logos, or pure and invariable presence in need of no explanation. Dependency theorists, just as the developmentalists they criticised, took for granted that development meant national development and growth. The image of the Western nation state took on a universalising role, quite divorced from the complexity and diversity of world history. Modernisation theory was based on an assumption about the smooth diffusion of European economic, political, social and cultural norms to the 'periphery'. We would argue that, while the radical dependency critique challenged the harmonious view of the world implicit in this diffusionist model, it shared its underlying assumption of history in terms of progress and linear temporality. To some extent, the radical critique of conservative development discourse, such as that contained in this book, tends simply to reverse the hierarchies they deal with (people versus profit, autonomous versus dependent growth, etc.) and does not move on to question their own ability to subvert logocentric reasoning.

Two contributions to this volume do begin to take us beyond the traditional dichotomies, namely those by Anderson and Goodman on Ireland's position within the European Community, and Cebulla and Smyth's analysis of post-Fordism in Belfast. The former argues that a 'Europe of the regions' will not replace the centrality of the nation state and the national conflict in Ireland. We would agree with their conclusion that: 'While regionalism is not displacing nationalism, its growth, and EC integration more generally, is perhaps the most important new factor affecting the national conflict.' Countering knee-jerk radical nationalist views in Ireland on the EC, one of us had similarly argued elsewhere that:

> National economic and political balances of power will in future increasingly be established within the wider framework of the EC. It is becoming less and less appropriate to rely exclusively on national mechanism to secure a democratic future. (Munck, 1993, p. 134)

As to the question of post-Fordism, as developed by Cebulla and Smyth, but also deployed by other contributors, it is, of course, one of the main themes of the post-Marxist or postmodernist theorists. Against cataclysmic views of the capitalist crisis, this school argues that we are entering a new era characterised by flexible working practices, a smaller role for trade unions, a reduction in state intervention, and a new individualism in social relations. The only word of caution here would be to point to the dangers of technological determinism inherent in this analysis, especially if applied unthinkingly to Ireland (Bonefeld and Holloway, 1991).

Gender Agendas

If there is one major flaw in most of the radical development discourse it is the conceptual and empirical blindness to the role and agency of women in the development process. Yet the control of women is central to all national development histories. The dynamics of gender are also central to post-colonial and nationalist discourses, nowhere more obviously than in Ireland. Gender is also crucially involved with questions of labour and of the state. The construction of women in patriarchal discourses is, at the same time, a construction of paid and unpaid labourers. Women are also central to state formation, as Kandiyoti argues, insofar as: 'Women bear the burden of being "mothers of the nation" ... as well as being those who reproduce the boundaries of ethnic/national groups, who transmit the culture and who are the privileged signifiers of national difference' (1993, p. 377). The regulation of gender should now be seen as central to the articulation of national identity and the national development process. The economic, social and political failings of most post-colonial regimes with regards to women force us to call into question the secular pretensions of nationalist movements and projects. In conclusion, a development discourse which does not focus on gender power and its relation to other forms of power is destined to become a 'malestream' discourse.

It is ironic that while feminism contributed to the impasse in development studies by constantly highlighting the 'invisibility of women' in development discourses, it also opens up ways forward. The theory and practice of feminism can help us break out of the deadlock in radical development theory in various ways. In her critical overview of the relationship between feminism and development theory, Kandiyoti (1993) highlights how recent debates have taken us beyond the 'Women in Development' school associated with the assumptions of the modernisation perspective. While the liberal 'Women in Development' school can be credited with bringing women into the development debate, it operated with an economic reductionist view which defined women as a coherent category in advance of their entry into the development process. The radical feminist development writers laid more stress on the complexity and diversity of the process whereby women were integrated into capitalist development. Nevertheless, they shared with their liberal counterparts a structuralist emphasis and a tendency towards universalising assumptions. Recent work has also tended to move away from the earlier views of women as helpless victims, buffeted by the forces of patriarchy, religion and tradition. Instead women are seen as prime agents within and around development projects, with their own diverse, and often contradictory, agendas.

Gender studies has, until recently, shared some of the problems associated with the use of meta-theories as deployed by conservative and radical development theories alike. The subsequent turn towards postmodernism, psychoanalysis and cultural studies led gender studies to a growing theoretical fragmentation and diversification. This would appear to be happening now within international development studies, where the problem has been, hitherto, the deeply held common assumptions of both conservative and radical variants. Poststructuralist feminism has helped move us beyond the binary oppositions based on sexual difference; men exploit, women are exploited. As Mohanty argues: 'Such simplistic formulations are historically reductive, they are also ineffectual in designing strategies to combat oppressions' (1993, p. 207). By analogy we should question the binary divisions deployed in radical development theories between centre and periphery, inward and outward looking development, dependent and autonomous, even development and underdevelopment. In terms of theoretical and practical challenges to the dominant development discourse, it is, arguably, women's movements which have been the most visible and challenging internationally. Parajuli puts the case that 'They may potentially offer an alternative framework not only for relations between men and women, but also for relations between humans and their environment, knowledge and power, the state and civil society' (1991, p. 177). That this challenge is still more of an aspiration than a reality should not prevent us from recognising its importance.

Transformation Time

Central to the poststructuralist debate is the notion of deconstruction. We have sought to question the assumptions of the Enlightenment discourse which saw progress as leading to harmonious development and the general emancipation of humankind. Deconstruction has led us to dismantling the structures and hidden assumptions of conservative and radical development discourses alike. The 'gender agenda' was the point of rupture we focused on in this deconstructive enterprise. It is necessary to follow through this critique to stress the need for self-sustaining growth which, arguably, also helps point the way out of the impasse in radical development theory. In the mid-1990s it is becoming increasingly clear that a new post-Fordist social compromise to replace the long-lasting Fordist one seems unlikely to materialise. Europe is certainly not the dynamic and democratic home envisaged by Jacques Delors in 1992. Lipietz (1992) has argued persuasively that an alternative development model is urgently needed, based on the values of solidarity, the autonomy of individuals and ecological responsibility. The emergence of new social movements articulating just such values has led to a sustained critique of the dominant development discourses and the productivist bias of mainstream and radical alternatives alike. Recognising that knowledge is a contested terrain, these movements, with their incipient but already noticeable effects in Ireland, are increasingly showing how developmentalist knowledge can be antithetical to people's interests.

Another point to pursue, following Tucker, is that: 'In development studies culture has tended to have been regarded as something of an epiphenomenon, secondary in importance to the all important economic and political domains' (1992, p. 2). For some time now, the work of Foucault has been taking development studies internationally beyond the narrow confines of economism. Foucault's insights into the (re)production of discourses and the relationship between knowledge and power, suggest interesting new ways to (re)interpret development theory and practice from a truly radical perspective. A Foucauldian perspective on development would begin by looking at the historical conditions, current deployment and techniques associated with the development discourse (Escobar, 1984). From this perspective, we can see how counter-discourses (such as radical development theory) have operated mainly within the same discursive space as the dominant strategy. This explains the ease with which the dominant development discourse has incorporated and neutralised so many 'radical' concepts such as human-centred, integrated or endogenous development. This does not mean that we should necessarily abandon the concept of development, but it does point towards the need to go beyond development as a unitary field of theory and practice. Following Said, Tucker argues that: 'Rethinking development in order to redress the problems posed [above] calls for a plurality of discourses, a plurality of audiences and a plurality of terrains' (1992, p. 24). We can but concur.

Finally, if it really is 'transformation time', as radicals making the new South Africa put it, we should probably ask again what development actually means. Even the solidly mainstream journal *World Development* now carries articles on 'the meaning of development' (Ingam, 1993). So the time seems ripe. Development discourse, so central to the Enlightenment, contains a metaphor of making visible what is already present. So, much as a photographic print is developed, we can reveal in the developing country what we already know to be there from the developed countries. That this interpretation is both evolutionary and reductionist should be clear by now. But this does not mean that we must necessarily accept the verdict of critics, such as Gustavo Esteva (1992), that 'development' has evaporated and that, after some decades, it is clear that this field of knowledge is a mined, unexplorable land. Though understandable, this desire seems somewhat premature and a rejection of Foucault's view of power as all-pervasive but eminently contestable. In Ireland there is actually a body of knowledge on the social and cultural, as well as the economic, aspects of development represented, for example, by the iconoclastic work of Lee (1989). One recent study, by Paul Keating and Derry Desmond, has in fact made a useful contribution to our understanding of the relationship between culture and capitalism in contemporary Ireland (Keating and Desmond, 1993). Also, recent work by Peadar Kirby points, if only in outline, to moves beyond the assimilationist and simple nationalist readings of Irish development (Kirby, 1993). A (re)construction of a radical democratic development discourse thus seems more appropriate to us than a premature evacuation of this terrain.

Conclusion

We should point out in conclusion that we are not seeking to advance a new 'postmodernist' orthodoxy in this field, but simply to recognise that the impasse in radical development studies is but one moment of a wider crisis of representation in the social sciences. Nor do we advocate a slide into some variant of postmodernist nihilism and uncritical celebration of difference. We do want to take the debate on development in Ireland out of the clutches of the crude bipolar structural opposition between 'centre' against 'periphery', which makes the latter a poor, tardy and stunted deviation from the normative centre (Richardson, 1993). If we look instead to the heterogeneity, plurality and contradictory nature of present-day Ireland we shall see instead many possibilities for transformation. A counter-hegemonic movement which is simply a mirror image of that which it seeks to transform will never succeed in this bid. Though this statement has obvious political implications – particularly regarding the nationalist discourse – which we cannot articulate here, it does bid us to question the apparently unquestionable truths underlying development discourses in Ireland.

Bibliography

Adams, G. (1986) *The Politics of Irish Freedom* (Dingle: Brandon).

Amin, S. (1974) *Accumulation on a World Scale: A Critique of the Theory of Underdevelopment* (New York: Monthly Review Press).

Amin, S. (1990) *Delinking: Towards a Polycentric World* (London: Zed Books).

Amin, S. (1992) 'Foreword' in Fawzy, M. (ed.) *The Arab World: Nation, State and Democracy* (Tokyo: United Nations University Press).

Anderson, B. (1989) *Imagined Communities* (London: Verso).

Anderson, J. (1993) 'The Political Significance of Northern Ireland's British Subvention'. Paper presented at the Economic Change and Development: Prospects for Peripheral Regions Conference. Queen's University Belfast (September).

Anderson, J. (1994) 'Problems of Inter-State Economic Integration: Northern Ireland and the Irish Republic in the European Community', *Political Geography*, vol. 1, no. 3.

Anderson, J. and Goodman, J. (1993) 'European Integration and the National Conflict in Ireland', in King, R. (ed.) *Ireland, Europe and the Single Market: Geographical Perspectives* (Dublin: Geography Society of Ireland Special Publications, no. 8).

Anderson, J. and Goodman, J. (1994) 'European and Irish Integration: Contradictions of Regionalism and Nationalism', *European Journal of Urban and Regional Studies*, vol. 2, no. 1.

Anderson, J. and Shuttleworth, I. (1992–3) 'Currency of Cooperation; and Bordering on the Difficult', *Fortnight*, no. 312.

Anon (1984) *Shankill Bulletin* (September).

Anon (1990) *Education for Mutual Understanding: A Warning to Protestant Parents* (Kilskeery: Free Presbyterian Church).

Association of County Councils (1992) 'The New Europe: Implications for UK Local Government', *ACC and Coopers Lybrand Deloitte*, Paper 7 (February).

Audit Commission (1991) *A Rough Guide to Europe: Local Authorities and the European Communities* (London: HMSO).

Balsom, D. (1990) 'Wales', in Watson, M. (ed.) *Contemporary Minority Nationalism* (London: Routledge).

Bank Ceannais na h Eireann (1992) *Irish Economic Statistics* (Dublin: Central Bank of Ireland).

Bateson, G. (1973) *Steps to an Ecology of Mind* (London: Paladin).

Belfast Regional Survey and Plan 1962 (1964) *Matthew Plan* (Belfast: HMSO).

Belfast Urban Area Plan (1987) (Belfast: HMSO).

Best, M.H. (1990) *The New Competition* (Cambridge: Polity Press).

Bew, P., Gibbon, P. and Patterson, H. (1979) *The State in Northern Ireland 1912–1972* (Manchester: Manchester University Press).

Birrell, D. and Wilson, C. (1993) 'Making Belfast Work: An Evaluation of an Urban Strategy', *Administration,* vol. 41, no. 1 (Spring).

Blair, T.L. (1973) *The Poverty of Planning* (London: Macdonald).

Bonefeld, W. and Holloway, J. (eds) (1991) *Post-Fordism and Social Form: A Marxist Debate on the Post-Fordist State* (London: Macmillan).

Bord Failte (1992) *'Developing Sustainable Tourism'. Tourism Development Plan 1993–97* (Dublin: Bord Failte).

Bord Failte (1993) *Choose Your Own Ireland* (London: Bord Failte).

Borooah, V.K. (1993) 'Northern Ireland: Typology of a Regional Eonomy', in Teague, P. (ed.) *The Economy of Northern Ireland: Perspectives for Structural Change* (London: Lawrence and Wishart).

Bradley, J., Fitzgerald, J. and Kearney, I. (1992) *The Role of the Structural Funds: Analysis of the Consequences for Ireland in the Context of 1992* (Dublin: Economic and Social Research Institute).

Bradley, J. and Wright, J. (1993) 'Two Regional Economies in Ireland'. Paper presented to a meeting of the Statistical and Social Inquiry Society of Ireland (May).

Bradshaw, B. (1989) 'Nationalism and Historical Scholarship in Modern Ireland', *Irish Historical Studies,* vol. 26.

Bradshaw, B. (1992) 'Interpretations of Irish History'. Paper presented at the 9th Irish Dimensions in British Education Conference (Leicester: Soar Valley College).

Brand, J. (1990) 'Scotland', in Watson, M. (ed.) *Contemporary Minority Nationalism* (London: Routledge).

Breathnach, P. (1988) 'Uneven Development and Capitalist Peripheralisation: The Case of Ireland', *Antipode*, vol. 20, no. 2.

Breathnach, P. (1993) 'European Industrial Investment in Ireland: A Geographical Perspective', in King, R. (ed.) *Ireland, Europe and the Single Market: Geographical Perspectives* (Dublin: Geography Society of Ireland Special Publications, No. 8).

Brown, S. (1985) 'City Centre Commercial Revitalisation: The Belfast Experience', *Planner* (June).

Brown, H. (1992) *Feminism and Development Theory: A Critical Overview* (Cork: Department of Sociology, Occasional Paper Series, no. 7).

Callen, T., Hannan, D.F., Nolan, B., Whelan, B.J. and Creighton, S. (1987) *Poverty and the Social Welfare System in Ireland* (Dublin: Combat Poverty Agency).

Callen, T., Nolan, B., Whelan, B.J., Hannon, D.F. and Creighton, S. (1989) *Poverty, Income and Welfare in Ireland* (Dublin: Economic and Social Research Institute).

Cameron, R. (1993) *Self-Determination? The Question Ulster Must Answer* (London: Ameron Press).

Cesaire, A. (1972) *Discourse on Colonialism* (New York: Monthly Review Press).

Chomney, L. (1993) 'The Political Significance of Faulty Governance'. Paper presented to the Social Change and Cultural Diversity Group. Queen's University Belfast (September).

Clulow, R. and Teague, P. (1993) 'Governance Structure and Economic Performance', in Teague, P. (ed.) *The Economy of Northern Ireland – Perspectives for Structural Change* (London: Lawrence and Wishart).

Cochrane, A. (1993) 'Beyond the Nation State? – Building the Euro-Region', in Bullmann, N. (ed.) *Die Politik der dritten Ebene Regionen im Prozess der E.* (Berlin: Nomos).

Colcough, C. and Manor, J. (eds) (1993) *States or Markets? Neo-Liberalism and the Development Policy Debate* (Oxford: Clarendon Press).

Commission of the European Communities (1984) *The Regions of the Enlarged Community: The Second Periodic Report on the Social and Economic Situation and Development of the Regions of the Community* (Luxembourg: Office for the Official Publications of the EC).

Commission of the European Communities (1989) *Guide to the Reform of the Community's Structural Funds* (Luxembourg: Commission of the European Communities).

Commission of the European Communities (1990) *The Regions of the Enlarged Community: The Fourth Periodic Report on the Social and Economic Situation and Development of the Regions of the Community* (Luxembourg: Office for the Official Publications of the EC).

Commission of the European Communities (1991) *Europe 2000: The Outlook for the Development of the Community's Territory* (Luxembourg: Office for the Official Publications of the EC).

Community Workers Cooperative (1992) *Structural Funds: The Challenge to Address Social Exclusion* (Dublin: Community Workers Cooperative).

Community Workers Cooperative (1993) *Making Submissions: An Evaluation of the Sub-Regional Review Committee Submissions in the Context of the CSF – The Influence of the Voluntary Community Sector* (Dublin: Community Workers Cooperative).

Connolly, J. (1973) *Selected Writings* (Harmondsworth: Penguin)

Corkery, K. (1967) *The Hidden Ireland* (Dublin: Gill and MacMillan).

Council of Europe (1988) *The Allocation of Powers to the Local and Regional Levels of Government in the Member States of the Council of Europe* (Strasbourg: Council of Europe Publications).

Crick, B. (1991) 'The English and the British', in Crick, B. (ed.) *National Identities* (London: Blackwell).

Crotty, R. (1986) *Ireland in Crisis: A Study in Capitalist Colonial Under-development* (Dingle: Brandon Books).

Curry, J. (1993) 'The Flexibility Fetish – A Review Essay on Flexible Specialisation', *Capital and Class*, no. 50 (Summer).

De Paor, L. (1970) *Divided Ulster* (Harmondsworth: Penguin).

Department of Enterprise and Employment (1993) *Employment Through Enterprise* (Dublin: Stationery Office).

Department of Finance (1992) *Community Support Framework and National Development Plan 1989–1993: Breakdown of Structural Spending All Sub-Regions* (Dublin: Department of Finance).

Department of Industry and Commerce (1990) *Review of Industrial Policy* (Dublin: Stationery Office).

DED (1987) *Building a Stronger Economy: The Pathfinder Process* (Belfast: Department of Economic Development).

DED (1990) *Competing in the 1990s: The Key to Growth* (Belfast: Department of Economic Development).

DSO (1990) *Local Government and Reform: Report of the Advisory Expert Committee* (the *Barrington Report*) (Dublin: Stationery Office).

DSO (1992a) *Ireland in Europe: A Shared Challenge: Economic Cooperation on the Island of Ireland in an Integrated Europe* (Dublin: Stationery Office).

DSO (1992b) *Report of the Industrial Policy Review Group* (the *Culliton Report*) (Dublin: Stationery Office).

Durkan, J. (1992) 'Social Consensus and Incomes Policy', *Economic and Social Review*, vol. 23, no. 3.

Economic and Social Research Institute (1993) *EC Structural Funds, the Community Support Framework: Evaluation and Recommendations* (Dublin: Economic and Social Research Institute).

Escobar, A. (1984) 'Discourse and Power in Development: Michel Foucault and the Relevance of his Work for the Third World', *Alternatives*, vol. 10 (Winter).

Esteva, G. (1992) 'Development', in Sachs, W. (ed.) *The Development Dictionary: A Guide to Knowledge as Power* (London: Zed Books).

European Commission (1992) *Second Survey of State Aids in the EC in the Manufacturing and Certain Other Sectors* (Brussels: European Commission).

European Parliament (1984) *Report Drawn up on Behalf of the Political Affairs Committee on the Situation in Northern Ireland* (the *Haagerrup Report*), *Parliamentary Working Documents*, nos. 1983–4 (Luxembourg: Working Document).

European Parliament (1991) *The Impact of 1992 and Associated Legislation on the Less Favoured Regions of the EC* (Luxembourg: Regional and Transport Series, no. 18).

European Parliament (1992) *Report to the Regional Policy Committee on Cross-Border and Inter-Regional Cooperation* (Luxembourg: Working Document, A301, August 8, 1992).

Fanon, F. (1967) *The Wretched of the Earth* (Harmondsworth: Penguin).

Fanon, F. (1970) *Black Skin, White Masks* (London: Paladin).

Farrell, M. (1976) *Northern Ireland: The Orange State* (London: Pluto Press).

Fenn, N. (1989) 'Britain, Ireland and European Integration', in Keogh, D. (ed.) *Ireland and the Challenge of Europe* (Cork: Hibernia University Press).

Fennell, D. (1993) *Heresy: The Battle of Ideas in Modern Ireland* (Belfast: Blackstaff).

Fitzgerald, G. (1991) *All in a Life: An Autobiography* (London: Macmillan).

Foley, A. (1991) 'The Export and Foreign Exchange Contribution of Overseas Industry', in Foley, A. and McAleese, D. (eds) *Overseas Industry in Ireland* (Dublin: Gill and Macmillan).

Foley, C. (1992) 'Fairness for All', *Irish Post* (July).

Freeman, J., Gaffikin, F. and Morrissey, M. (1987) *Making the Economy Work: An Alternative Strategy* (Belfast: Amalgamated Transport and General Workers Union).

Gerschenkron, A. (1962) *Economic Backwardness in a Historical Perspective* (Cambridge: Harvard University Press).

Gibbons, L. (1988) 'Coming Out of Hibernation? The Myth of Modernity in Irish Culture', in Kearney, R. (ed.) *Across the Frontiers: Ireland in the 1990s* (Dublin: Wolfhound Press).

Gordon, I. (1990) 'Regional Policies and National Politics in Britian', *Environment and Planning: Government and Politics*, vol. 8.

Gorz, A. (1989) *Critique of Economic Reason* (London: Verso).

Government Information Services (1989) 'Reynolds Outlines Community Support Framework' (Press Release, November).

Government of Ireland (1989) *Ireland: National Development Plan 1989–1993* (Dublin: Stationery Office).

Government of Ireland (1993) *Ireland: National Development Plan 1994–1999* (Dublin: Stationery Office).

Greenslade, L. (1991) 'A Culture of Madness? Schizophrenia in Modern Ireland'. Paper presented at the 5th Workshop in Social Science Research (University of Liverpool).

Griffin, K. and Gurley, G. (1985) 'Radical Analyses of Imperialism, the Third World, and the Transition to Socialism: A Survey Article', *Journal of Economic Literature* , vol. 23 (September).

Gudgin, G. (1992) 'Avoiding the Worst: Northern Ireland in Recession', *Irish Banking Review* (Winter).

Hamilton, D. (1993) 'Foreign Investment and Industrial Development in Northern Ireland', in Teague, P. (ed.) *The Economy of Northern Ireland: Perspectives for Structural Change* (London: Lawrence and Wishart).

Harris, R.I.D., Jefferson, C.W. and Spencer, J.E. (eds) (1990) *The Northern Ireland Economy* (Harlow: Longman).

Hart, M. and Harrison, R. (1992) 'Northern Ireland', in Martin, R. and Townroe, P. (eds) *Regional Development in the 1990's* (London: Jessica Kingsley).

Hayton, K. (1992) *Local Economic Development and Scottish Local Government Reform* (Manchester: The Planning Exchange).

Henderson, J. (1990) 'The Role of the State in the Four NICs'. Paper to conference 'The Growth Economies of Asia', University of Keele, September.

Hitchens, D.M.W.N., Wagner, K. and Birnie, J.E. (1990) *Closing the Productivity Gap* (Aldershot: Avebury).

ICTU (1993) *New Forms of Work Organisation: Options for Unions* (Dublin: Irish Congress of Trade Unions).

IDB (1990) *Forward Strategy 1991–93* (Belfast: Industrial Development Board).

Industrial Policy Review Group (1992) *A Time for Change: Industrial Policy for the 1990s* (Dublin: The Stationery Office).

Ingam, B. (1993) 'The Meaning of Development: Interaction Between "New" and "Old" Ideas', *World Development*, vol. 21, no. 11.

Isles, K. and Cuthbert, N. (1957) *An Economic Survey of Northern Ireland* (Belfast: HMSO).
ITGWU (1981–8) *Industrial Development* (Dublin: Irish Transport and General Workers Union).
Jacobson, D. and Andreosso, B. (1990) 'Ireland as a Location for Multinational Investment', in Foley, A. and Mureaney, M. (eds) *The Single European Market and the Irish Economy* (Dublin: Institute of Public Administration).
Jameson, F. (1981) *The Political Unconscious* (London: Methuen).
Kandyoti, D. (1993) 'Identity and its Discontents: Women and the Nation', in Williams, P. and Chrisman, L. (eds.) *Colonial Discourse and Post-Colonial Theory* (London: Harvester Wheatsheaf).
Keane, Colm (1993) (ed.) *The Jobs Crisis* (Cork: RTE/Mercier).
Keating, M. (1988) *State and Regional Nationalism: Territorial Politics and the European State* (London: Harvester).
Keating, P. and Desmond, D. (1993) *Culture and Capitalism in Contemporary Ireland* (Aldershot: Avebury).
Keatinge, P. (1987) 'Irish Foreign Relations in 1986', *Irish Studies in International Affairs,* vol. 2, no. 3.
Keeble, D., Owens, P.L. and Thompson, C. (1982) 'Regional Accessibility and Economic Potential in the European Community', *Regional Studies,* vol. 16, no. 6.
Kennedy, K.A. (1992) 'Real Convergence, the European Community and Ireland', *Statistical and Social Enquiry Society of Ireland* (May).
Kennedy, K.A. (1993a) 'Long-term Trends in the Irish Economy', *Irish Banking Review* (Summer).
Kennedy, K.A. (1993b) 'The Unemployment Crisis in Ireland', *Undercurrents* (Cork: Cork University Press).
Kennedy, K.A., Giblin, T. and McHugh, D. (1988) *The Economic Development of Ireland in the 20th Century* (London: Routledge).
Kenny, V. (1985) 'The Post-Colonial Personality', *Crane Bag,* vol. 9.
Kirby, P. (1988) *Has Ireland a Future?* (Cork: Mercier).
Kirby, P. (1993) 'Challenging Passivity', *Irish Reporter,* no. 12.
Laffan B. (1989) 'While you're over there in Brussels, get us a Grant: The Management of EC Funding in Ireland', *Irish Political Studies,* vol. 4, nos. 43–57.
LEDU (1991) *Forward Thinking: LEDU's Corporate Plan 1989–1994* (Belfast: Local Enterprise Development Unit).
Lee, J.J. (1989) *Ireland 1912–1985: Politics and Society* (Cambridge: Cambridge University Press).
Lipietz, A. (1992) *Towards a New Economic Order: Postfordism, Ecology and Democracy* (Cambridge: Polity Press).

Loughlin, J. (1991) 'The Anglo-Irish Agreement: Federal Arrangement or Affirmation of the Nation-State?' *Federalisme*, vol. 3, nos. 183–97.

MacKay, R. (1992) '1992 and Relations with the EEC', in Martin, R. and Townroe, P. (eds) *Regional Development in the 1990s* (London: Jessica Kingsley).

McAleese, D.F. (1993) 'The Micro Economic Framework', in Gray, A.W. (ed.) *Response to Irish Unemployment* (Dublin: Indecon).

McAuley, J. (1991) 'Cuchullainn and an RPG–7: The Ideology and Politics of the Ulster Defence Associtiion', in Hughes, E. (ed.) *Culture and Politics in Northern Ireland* (Milton Keynes: Open University Press).

McAuley, J. (1994) *The Politics of Identity* (Aldershot: Avebury).

McCluskey, R. (1994) *Ireland's Crisis* (Belfast: Harper Press).

McGimpsey, C. (1993) 'The Economic Impossibility of a United Ireland'. Paper presented to the Irish Association (Dublin).

Macro Economic Research Group (1993) *Making Democracy Work: A Framework for Macroeconomic Policy in South Africa* (South Africa: Centre for Development Studies).

Malecki, E. (1991) *Technology and Economic Development* (Harlow: Longman).

Mannoni, O. (1964) *Prospero and Caliban: The Psychology of Colonization* (New York: Praeger).

Mansour, F. (1992) *The Arab World: Nation, State and Democracy* (Tokyo: United Nations University Press).

Manzo, K. (1991) 'Modernist Discourse and the Crisis of Development Theory', *Studies in Comparative International Development*, vol. 26, no. 2.

Martinos, H. (1989) *The Management of Local Employment Development Strategies* (London: South Bank Technopark).

Marshall, A. (1920) *Principles of Economics*, 8th edn (London: Macmillan).

Martinelli, F. and Schoenberger, E. (1991) 'Oligopoly is Alive and Well: notes for a broader discussion of flexible accumulation', in Benko, G. and Dunford, M. (eds) *Industrial Change and Regional Development* (London: Belhaven).

Marx, K. and Engels, F. (1970) *The German Ideology* (London: Lawrence and Wishart).

Mayers, B. (1989) 'Restructuring and Popular Opposition in West German Cities', in Smith, M.P. and Feagin, J.E. (eds) *The Capitalist City* (Oxford: Oxford University Press).

Meldon, J. (1992) *Structural Funds and the Environment: Problems and Prospects* (Dublin: An Taisce).

Memmi, A. (1965) *The Coloniser and the Colonised* (New York: Orion).

Miller, R.L., Osborne, R.D., Cormack, R.J. and Williamson, A.P. (1987) 'Higher Education and Labour Market Entry: The Differing Experiences of Northern Irish Protestants and Catholics'. Paper presented at Nuremberg Meeting of the International Sociological Association, Social Stratification Research Committee (April).

Mjoset, L. (1992) *The Irish Economy in a Comparative Institutional Perspective* (Dublin: National Economic and Social Council Report, no. 93).

Mohanty, C.T. (1993) 'Under Western Eyes: Feminist Scholarship and Colonial Discourses', in Williams, P. and Chrisman, L. (eds) *Colonial Discourse and Post-Colonial Theory* (London: Harvester Wheatsheaf).

Moser, C. (1989) 'Gender Planning in the Third World. Meeting Practical and Strategic Gender Needs', *World Development*, vol. 17, no. 11.

Munck, R. (1993) *The Irish Economy: Results and Prospects* (London: Pluto Press).

Munck, R. (1994) 'Democracy and Development: Deconstruction and Debates', in Sklair, L. (ed.) *Capitalism and Development* (London: Macmillan).

Myrdal, G. (1957) *Economic Theory and Underdeveloped Regions* (London: Duckworth).

Myrdal, G. (1973) 'Crises and Cycles in the Development of Economics', *Political Quarterly* , vol. 44.

Nairn, T. (1977) *The Break-Up of Britain* (London: New Left Books).

National Economic and Social Forum (1993) *National Development Plan 1994–1999 – The Proposed Local Development Programme, Forum Report No. 2* (Dublin: Stationery Office).

NESC (1989) *Ireland in the European Community: Performance, Prospects and Strategy* (Dublin: National Economic and Social Council, no. 88).

NESC (1992) *Women's Participation in the Irish Labour Market* (Dublin: National Economic and Social Council, no. 94).

NIEC (1991) *Economic Strategy in Northern Ireland* (Belfast: Northern Ireland Economic Council, no. 88).

NIEC (1992) *Inward Investment in Northern Ireland* (Belfast: Northern Ireland Economic Council, no. 99).

NIEC (1993) *Transport Infrastructure and Policy in Northern Ireland* (Belfast: Northern Ireland Economic Council, no. 104).

NIERC (1993a) *Government Grants and Manufacturing Profitability in Northern Ireland* (Belfast: Northern Ireland Economic Research Centre).

NIERC (1993b) *Training, Skills and Company Competitiveness: A Comparison of Matched Plants in Northern Ireland and Germany* (Belfast: Northern Ireland Economic Research Centre).

O'Donnell, R. (1993) *Ireland and Europe: Challenges for a New Century* (Dublin: Economic and Social Research Institute).

O'Dowd, L. (1992) 'Borders in the New Europe'. Paper presented to the TCD Department of Sociology Colloquium (November).

O'Dowd, L., Rolston, B. and Tomlinson, M. (1980) *Northern Ireland: Between Civil Rights and Civil War* (London: CSE Books).

O'Hearn, D. (1993) 'Global Competition, Europe and Irish Peripherality', *Economic and Social Review*, vol. 24, no. 2.

O'Leary B., et al. (1993) *Northern Ireland: Sharing Authority* (London, IPPR).

O'Malley, E. (1989) *Industry and Economic Development: The Challenge of the Latecomer* (Dublin: Gill and Macmillan).

O'Toole, F. (1990) *A Mass for Jesse James* (Dublin: Raven Arts Press).

OECD (1993) *Economic Survey Ireland* (Paris: Organization for Economic Cooperation and Development).

Oldham, C.H. (1914) 'The Incidence of Emigration on Town and Country Life in Ireland', *Journal of the Social and Statistical Enquiry Society of Ireland*, vol. 13.

Parajuli, P. (1991) 'Power and Knowledge in Development Discourse: New Social Movements and the State in India', *International Social Science Journal*, no. 127.

Patterson, H. (1989) *The Politics of Illusion* (London: Hutchinson).

Peet, R. (1991) *Global Capitalism: Theories of Societal Development* (London: Routledge).

Perrons, D.C. (1981) 'The Role of Ireland in the New International Division of Labour: A Proposed Framework for Regional Analysis' *Regional Studies*, vol. 15.

Perrons, D.C. (1992) 'The Region and the Single Market', in Dunford, M. and Kafkalas, G. (eds) *Cities and Regions in the New Europe* (London: Belhaven).

Perroux, F. (1955) 'Note sur la notion de "pole de croissance" ', *Economie Appliquée*, vol. 8.

Piore, M. and Sabel, C. (1984) *The Second Industrial Divide* (New York: Basic Books).

Porter, M.E. (1990) *The Competitive Advantage of Nations* (London: Macmillan).

Portz, J. (1993) 'State Economic Development Programs: The Trials and Tribulations of Implementation', *Economic Development Quarterly*, vol. 7, no. 2 (May).
PPRU (1987) *Transport Costs in Peripheral Regions, Occasional Paper 7* (Belfast: Department of Finance and Personnel).
PPRU (1988) *1977 Belfast Areas of Need: Updated by 1981 Census Results* (Belfast: Policy Planning and Research Unit).
PPRU (1993) 'Continuous Household Survey', *PPRU Monitor*, no. 1/93.
Quigley, G. (1992) 'Ireland – an Island Economy'. Speech to the Confederation of Irish Industry, Dublin (February).
Reynolds, A. (1991) 'Ireland's Role in the EC: A Financial Perspective' (Press Release).
Richardson, H.W. (1969) *Regional Economics* (London: Weidenfeld and Nicolson).
Richardson, N. (1993) 'Postmodernism and Periphery', in Docherty, T. (ed.) *Postmodernism: A Reader* (London: Harvester Wheatsheaf).
Rowthorn, B. (1987) 'Northern Ireland: An Economy in Crisis', in Teague, P. (ed.) *Beyond the Rhetoric* (London: Lawrence and Wishart).
Rowthorn, B. and Wayne, N. (1988) *Northern Ireland: The Political Economy of Conflict* (Cambridge: Polity Press).
Said, E. (1993) *Culture and Imperialism* (London: Vintage).
Schoenberger, E. (1990) 'US Manufacturing Investments in Western Europe: Markets, Corporate Strategy and the Competitive Environment', *Annals of the Association of American Geographers*, vol. 80, no. 3.
Scott, A.J. and Storper, M. (1990) 'Regional Development Reconsidered', *Working Paper no. 1* (Los Angeles: Lewis Center for Regional Policy Studies).
Schuurman, F. (ed.) (1993) *Beyond the Impasse: New Directions in Development Theory* (London: Zed Books).
Sen, A. (1989) 'Food and Freedom', *World Development*, vol. 17, no. 6.
Shirlow, P. (1994) 'A Perspective on Irish Development', *Irish-European Studies*, vol. 6, no. 2.
Shirlow, P. and Shuttleworth, I. (1994) 'Training, Migration and the Changing World Order: A Case Study from the Republic of Ireland', in Gould, W. and Finlay, A. (eds) *Population Migration and the Changing World Order* (Chichester: Wiley).
Shriver, L. (1993) 'Role Reversals', *Forthnight* (April).

Sklair, L. (1988) 'Foreign Investment and Irish Development: A Study of the International Division of Labour in the Mid-West Region of Ireland', *Progress in Planning* , vol. 29.

Smyth, J. (1988) 'Stretching the Boundaries: The Control of Dissent in Northern Ireland', *Terrorism*, no. 2.

Smyth, J. (1991) 'Industrial Development and the Unmaking of the Irish Working Class', in Hutton, S. and Stewart, P. (eds) *Ireland's Histories* (London: Routledge).

Storper, M. and Walker, R. (1989) *The Capitalist Imperative: Territory, Technology and Industrial Growth* (Oxford: Basil Blackwell).

Summers, A. (1975) *Damned Whores and God's Police: The Colonization of Women in Australia* (Harmondsworth: Penguin).

Sweeney, P. (1990) *The Politics of Public Enterprise and Privatisation* (Dublin: Tomar).

Sweeney, P. (1991) 'The Employment Effects of the Commercialisation of Irish Public Enterprise', *Labour Market Review* (Summer).

Sweeney, P. (1992) 'A Response to Culliton', *Statistical and Social Enquiry Society of Ireland* (June).

Taylor, P. (1983) *The Limits of European Integration* (London: Croom Helm).

Teague, P. (ed.) (1993a) *The Economy of Northern Ireland: Perspectives for Structural Change* (London: Lawrence and Wishart).

Teague, P. (1993b) 'The Northern Ireland Economy: A Time for Institutional Change', *Local Economy*, vol. 7, no. 4.

Telesis Consultancy Group (1982) *A Review of Industrial Policy* (Dublin: National Economic and Social Council, report no. 64).

Tovery, H., Hannon, D. and Abramson, H. (1989) *Why Irish? Language and Identity in Ireland Today* (Baile Atha Cliath: Bord na Gaeilge).

Trimble, M.J. (1990) 'The Impact of the European Community', in Harris, R.I.D., et al. (eds) *The Northern Ireland Economy* (Harlow: Longman).

Tucker, V. (1992) *The Myth of Development* (Cork: Department of Sociology, Occasional Paper series, no. 6).

Vandamme, J. (1981) 'Regionalism in Europe', in Demeron, D. (ed.) *Regionalism and Supranationalism* (London: Political Studies Association).

Volsinov, V.N. (1973) *Marxism and the Philosophy of Language* (New York: Seminar Press).

Walsh, B.M. (1993) 'Appropriate Policy Changes', in Gray, A.W. (ed.) *Responses to Irish Unemployment* (Dublin: Indecon).

Walsh, F. (1979) 'The Changing Industrial Structures of Northern and Southern Ireland', *Maynooth Review*, vol. 5, no. 2.
Walsh, J.A. (ed.) (1991) *Local Economic Development and Administrative Reform* (Dublin: Regional Studies Association).
Walsh, J.A. (1993) 'Regional Development in Ireland under the Community Support Framework: Review and Prospects', in Van der Kamp, H. (ed.) *EC Funds for Ireland: Getting it Right* (Dublin: Regional Studies Association).
Walsh, J.A. (1993) 'Planning for Local and Regional Development in Ireland', *Irish Banking Review* (Autumn).
Waters, J. (1991) *Jiving at the Crossroads* (Belfast: Blackstaff).
Wiener, R. (1980) *The Rape and Plunder of the Shankill* (Belfast: Farset).
Wilden, A. (1987a) *Man and Woman, War and Peace: The Strategist's Companion* (London: Routledge and Kegan Paul).
Wilden, A. (1987b) *The Rules are No Game: The Strategy of Communication* (London: Routledge and Kegan Paul).

Index

Published by Pluto Press

War and an Irish Town

Eamonn McCann

[illegible]

'There is no one who can [illegible] the way in which McCann [illegible] the events of those early years of the Troubles.'

Robert Fisk, [illegible]

[illegible]

Dominic [illegible]

[illegible]

Suspect Community

[illegible]

[illegible] Prevention of Terrorism Acts [illegible]

[illegible]

[illegible]

[illegible]

[illegible]

[illegible]

Pluto Press

345 Archway Road, London N6 5AA

140 Commerce Street, East Haven, CT 06512, USA